Once Upon
a Time
in Production

Once Upon a Time in Production

Jacques Bidou

In collaboration with
Marianne Dumoulin

Translated by Holly Aylett

ISBN 978-1-942782-94-0

Cinema as a witness, a place for debate, learning, reflection and emotion. This is the project that Jacques Bidou has been orchestrating since 1987, from the heart of his company, JBA Production, which I joined in 1992.

To produce engaged, committed work across a large number of countries is particularly complex, especially today. Support available to European productions (in this case, French) is often essential for financing, for the freedom to write and direct, and for exhibition. With this support, we have produced 114 films: 72 documentaries and 42 feature films, mainly from the Global South, including *Site 2*, *Rice People*, *One Evening after the War* by Cambodian filmmaker Rithy Panh; *Salt of this Sea* and *Wajib* by Palestinian filmmaker Annemarie Jacir; *Salvador Allende* by Chilean Patricio Guzman; four feature films—*Bab el-Oued City*, *Salut Cousin!*, *The Repentant* and *The Rooftops*—by Algerian filmmaker Merzak Allouache; *Face and Wandering Dogs* by Malaysian-Taiwanese Tsai Ming-Liang; *April Captains* by Portuguese director Maria de Medeiros; *Lumumba* by Haitian filmmaker Raoul Peck and *Donbass* by Ukrainian filmmaker Sergei Loznitsa, not to mention the first works of Chilean filmmaker Fernando Guzzoni, *Dog Flesh* and *Jesus*; Argentinean Pablo Agüero's *Salamandra* and *Eva Doesn't Sleep*; Iranian Massoud Bakhshi's *A Respectable Family* and *Yalda, a Night for Forgiveness*; Hungarian *Marcell Gero, Cain's Children*; and Italian Alice Rohwacher's *Corpo Celeste*.

The list is long: 114 films from more than 25 filmmakers (half of them first-time directors, from a variety of countries), all of which have been screened at major festivals and won numerous awards. An impressive filmography, but one that still leaves us in an uncomfortable, even precarious, situation. The profession of producer remains poorly understood and, in many respects, scorned and envied, not to say unloved.

It was time for Jacques to take up his pen and to tell the story, with suspense and a touch of humour, of the ups and downs of producing films from the ends of the earth, the bumpy, chaotic and often epic journeys, taking as an overall structure the production of the feature film *Yalda, a Night for Forgiveness*, from birth to its consecration at the Sundance Film Festival. It was time to place the producer at the centre of the story and reach people's hearts, with integrity and judgement. The time had come to tell it like it is.

A brief account of our career pathways, the experiences that informed our choice of profession as producers, is useful background.

Jacques, a gardian in the Camargue, spends his days on horseback rather than in school, which perhaps explains his love of Westerns. He eventually passes his baccalaureate through a correspondence course and joins the Department of Direction at INSAS, the film school in Belgium's French-speaking community. Then came the meeting with Marker[*]

---

[*] Chris Marker (1921-2012). Filmmaker, photographer, philosopher, essayist, critic, poet and inspiration for an entire generation.

and the great era of political engagement: the general strike of May '68 and its occupied factories, Les Etats Généraux du Cinéma,* the companies Dynadia and Unicité, ten years of production within the sphere of the Communist Party, and then, in 1987, the creation of JBA Production.

I joined JBA in 1992 as a young mother, with no training but some production experience, notably at CDN Production, with the indomitable Gilles Sandoz. I worked in the development laboratory at the time the S16mm Aaton was created by the brilliant Beauviala and as queen of end-of-shoot parties. At JBA I progress from being in charge of reception at the rue de Turenne offices to overseeing post-production and then rapidly take on executive production of the feature films. It's exhilarating. Film after film, one after another, from Algiers to Lisbon, from Harare to Beira, from Joburg to Bissau.

In 1999, Jacques pushed me to undertake EAVE, a training course for producers, but I was reluctant— too much work, poor English, no time. But the magic of the clear Finnish nights and the noisy English bars would lead me to the script for *A Piece of Sky*. Women's words. Prison Factory. The first feature film by Belgian filmmaker Bénédicte Liénard. It was the trigger. I want to produce this project, to accompany it from screenplay to its release. Severine Caneele and Sofia Leboutte, Yolande Moreau, Josiane Stoléru, André Wilms and Olivier Gourmet in the cast, Hélène Louvart as director of photography, Marie-Hélène Dozo as editor, Ferran and Laforce

---

* The General Assembly of French Cinema brought together filmmakers, technicians, critics and others from the French cinema industry to address pressing issues and align itself with broader social and political movements.

on sound. A masterful team. Location shoots in a prison and a factory. A powerful film. We will walk the red carpet of Cannes with Béné, just behind Brad Pitt. We will devour mayo chips with our feet in the Mediterranean, our backs to the Majestic, staring out at the horizon with the crew and Bella, the actress serving a prison sentence during production, still under the yoke of double jeopardy.*

The birth of a unique collaboration between Jacques and I. Our differences—gender, age, personal backgrounds—were and continue to be our strength. Always in synergy on the substance, but always with our distinctive approaches. Quarrels too, often linked to the machismo and misogyny of people we deal with, of which I am the victim. A man over the age of twenty remains for many the superior, even among those who claim to be fervent defenders of the feminist cause. Jacques is often celebrated and I am called in to solve problems. Some of our partners find it difficult to have a female boss. I take it. I get enraged and sometimes explode in anger. There is still a long way to go.

We form a duo who work together on the same films in harmony and with transparency. Nomadic craftsmen, we continue to develop projects, to translate the scripts, to juggle the budgets, to keep up with technological innovations (we've come a long way since the days of flatbed editing machines and Éclair cameras) and to stick as close as possible to these projects in order to understand and shepherd

---

* Beatrice Spiga, a Belgian of Italian origin, was released from jail after post-production but then immediately charged with deportation under the law of double jeopardy. Thanks to the director, Bénédicte Liénard, she was eventually allowed to remain in Belgium.

them. Two people are stronger than one when keeping your head and not giving in.

JBA's production office—modest but full of charm—is in Belleville. It's important to care about where you live. We also have this in common; the beauty of place, the calibre of wine and the taste of food. Both curious and gourmet, sometimes too much so. We are committed to tackling major issues from the inside and taking on urgent subjects. Alongside the moments of happiness and light in these engagements, we also need determination, courage and the imagination to take on the injustices, the wounds, still open, from the past. The wounds are deep, the darkness immense. We will not always come back unscathed but we will be nourished by these immersions, artistic and human, enlarged by all these encounters.

You can enjoy reading *Once Upon a Time in Production*, whether you are from the film world, aspiring to enter it or from a completely different walk of life. You can read it without having seen *Yalda, a Night for Forgiveness*, although our hope is that it will make you curious to discover it. This account is above all a thrilling dive into the palpitating world of production.

Marianne Dumoulin

To the filmmakers,
who are the heart of it

This morning S called to tell us that she was closing our account. Just the one for our film, *Yalda*. We could use the others, no problem. We had been a customer of this bank for 29 years, but with a click—just like that—she had closed that account. Since JBA started, one of our main principles has been loyalty. A fine word it is. We use it at every turn, with suppliers, banks, partners. Loyalty is always a priority. In reality, it's meaningless, and sometimes even backfires. Our partners, with rare exceptions, disappear and change shop, and the memory of what has happened, of our own integrity, only stays lodged in our minds, in accordance with our values—foolishly, but not those of a bank or a large laboratory.

It should be noted that the time for "humanity" in relations in our sector has disappeared, body and soul. The time for exchange between people with a common goal of working together to find solutions has been swept away by the logic of these large companies, overdetermined by economics, where human and cultural aspects increasingly go down the drain. This is a disease quickly contracted by institutions subject to the criteria and pressures of the private sector. The turnover of intermediaries is so volatile. They are barely identified before they escape, especially the best, who climb up then disappear just when we've started to build trust in them. These intermediaries increasingly depend on computerised systems for processing all requests. Online labyrinth of procedures, machines, press 1, press the star button…

That morning of the 20th of February, I call the CNC.[4] A delicious welcome: "CNC, good morning, an operator will be with you shortly." Then comes the gentle voice of the great musician Michel Legrand—he has just left us, dear Michel—with whom I have the privilege of spending three minutes, albeit intercut by horrible scratchy noises, probably due to the loop. Finally, the operator kindly intercepts. "Good morning, can you put me through… Hold the line." Then, as is almost always the case, I get an answering machine and this time an elaborate message: "Hello, I'm out of town from the 16th of July to the 3rd of August, please call back later." It is now the 20th of February. I call back, wait again. Michel is still there in the background, and the operator connects me to another answering machine: "We are unavailable until the 16th of February." This time we are getting closer; it's only four days later. I call back a third time and tell the operator about my misfortunes. She sympathises and ends up finding someone who does answer but who isn't from the right department. I insist, gently, that he find me someone available in the relevant department. I sense I'm seriously annoying him but he doesn't lose his temper and finally I get through to someone available in the department who replies, curtly, "Everything is on our site. Read it carefully and call back if you have specific questions."

The CNC. Times have changed a lot. Those days when we had allies, committed to our side, available, defending cinema. Those meetings with Jean-Luc

---

[4] French National Centre of Cinema and Animation, CNC, responsible for production and promotion of cinema and audiovisual arts in France.

Douat* where, with his time-consuming sense of humour, we would search together for solutions to the potential production approvals, essential to the life of a film. He would mockingly turn to his big cupboard, a cave for all the improprieties of French cinema, and grab the file he called Affaires Bidou. Our projects turned out to be eternal brain teasers challenging the imbroglio of the points system.† It was so clear that we were making films that in no way ran counter to the interests of French cinema. But today the institution declares itself "against," especially against the myriad producers who devour public money, incapable of exceeding four hundred thousand admissions at the box office.

We learn of the disappearance of the Éclair group. A whole history collapses. A factory in Epinay with its chemistry, its smells, the melted snow on its gravel paths in winter, its work teams, the long-term friendships. Madam M, to whom we offered corrupting chocolates to get our negative edit to the top of the pile during a Cannes emergency. We rode our motorbikes day after day, the road impassable for four-wheeled vehicles, risking our lives, daredevils on the perilous ring road, to watch the rushes of a serene shoot in far-off Cambodia. A factory full of women, men, the lives of cinema, now scattered, theoretically reborn in the chilly realm of digital technology. Cultures that struggle to translate. An integrity built up during those long sessions of engagement, confrontation, incomprehension and animated discussion after the screenings.

---

* Jean-Luc Douat, then head of the film department at CNC.
† With rare exceptions, in order to exist and access funding, films need a production agreement from the CNC.

Precious experiences are dissolving. It's not a question of nostalgia, more a state of crisis, the race for profitability, the return on assets. Skills are withering away, ever faster, more fragmented. Change is accelerating, transmission of skills is no longer possible, programmes are eliminating the learning links: exit the trainees and assistants. A rift now between generations that no longer speak exactly the same language. And in the midst of all this we receive this friendly e-mail from our bank: "How to develop your cyber security," no doubt preparing us to arm ourselves against cyber attacks from Iran.

The Grand Hotel

We get together in Cannes, an apartment with a terrace on the 9th floor of the Grand Hotel. The Bank has transformed into a real beehive—buffet, champagne—and once again, with our usual enthusiasm, we tell the long and beautiful story of this project, another complicated one, suddenly placed under the lens of a dangerous character named Trump. But we think we have allies, almost friends at times. They listen to us, get engrossed, get worried. Then they return to Paris and there, in their sealed and, it must be said, sinister meeting rooms, they take sweet revenge for such dreariness, take back control, and, following a pathetic interview, decide to kick us out. A lesson in geopolitics from an aristocratic head of department: "Politicians can flex their muscles with Trump but not the business world." "What are you going to do in Iran? No industrialist, no bank, will take the risk of being unable to trade with the United States, of no longer working with the dollar." "No, sorry, we have no choice. It has already cost us a lot. We cannot take the slightest risk." A diabolically clear message, and what has become of that Iranian cinema that delights the whole of Cannes?

A courtier's profession. They love us so long as things are going well, so long as we keep them in the limelight, but as soon as there is the slightest hitch there is no mercy. We are being wooed and we must like all those who finance us. We have to seduce, to woo in our turn. Jean-André Fieschi* offered to record my telephone conversations with those we strive to seduce and convince, for just one day, so that I could listen back to myself. A bitter experience. It takes enormous conviction, a sacred sense of commitment and cinema, to sustain us in this role. It's the price we pay to do what we do every day.

We engage deeply with each filmmaker to draw out certain fundamentals, those you find when you're with someone who's going to surprise you, from whom there's a lot to learn, who is stronger than we are, and with whom we can embark on this small sailboat for a four- to six-year tour round the world. All the other passengers will be able to stop off and disappear along the way, except for this filmmaker and ourselves. We run into difficult times, failures, wear and tear, doubts; it's never straightforward. It's therefore necessary to ensure the quality of the "fuel" that will sustain us and, above all, commit ourselves to someone who is profoundly "trustworthy." The ethical dimension of our profession remains undoubtedly the most important. The road is long, increasingly long, and full of pitfalls.

In the early years, we read everything, watched the films. It was a time when we might receive one or

---

* Jean-Andre Fieschi. Writer, filmmaker, a dear friend—now departed.

two scripts a week, the paper era. It is easy to forget
that we have gone from 16mm double strip projection
to half-inch tape, from U-matic to VHS, then to
DVD, already outdated. There are no more DVD
drives in our computers. We are simply connected,
the world available at our fingertips. The changes
over the last thirty years have been meteoric. Distant
and diffuse memories of the crackling of the telex at
the entrance of our offices on rue de Turenne at the
end of the 1980s; the first portable computers for
individual use, the 'Amstrads'; the very first Mac; the
first appearance of the web with the Minitel; the first
satellite telephones that weighed a kilo; a revolution
called fax; the proliferation of computer uses and the
switch to a new universe; the standardisation of the
mobile phone condensed into a 'smartphone'; the
disappearance of the fax, the appearance of the scan;
the transmission of sound and image data across the
planet; teleconferencing, Zoom, Skype, the retreat of
direct contacts; the Internet and artificial intelligence;
the click as a remedy for all failures. And every day
of our lives starts by reading emails, answering them,
cleaning up spam and being engulfed in the silence of
social networking. And everyone now to be connected
by being face to face with their mobile phone.

So we were reading everything. In the pit of
our stomachs the nightmare of exhausting evenings,
weekends, holidays, with most of the time taken up
by bad scripts and films which deprive us of the joy
of indulging in reading books or seeing films, good
ones. A deadly drift, made worse by the fact of a
professional identity which is still unstable, one which
succumbs to an avalanche of everything and anything.

1987: South African Chronicles

We have to make clear choices that deeply reflect our aims and convictions. Building an identity takes time. A film takes between four and five years, and it takes a few films to get established. Ours materialised quite quickly. Our very first film, in 1987, *South African Chronicles*,* summed up the essence of our quest. Young South African filmmakers immersed in the different communities, translating the cruelty and violence of a system, an insider's eye, a documentary. We intervened in a situation of urgency, producing the country's young filmmakers (almost half of our productions have been first films), allowing time to research, to learn, time to shoot, to edit. It was around these choices that the team comes together, prepared to stand up for this kind of approach. At the time we were privileged to meet magnificent creative commissioning editors from the channels: Arte (then called "La Sept"), ZDF in Germany, Channel 4 in the United Kingdom, and a few others in Italy, Spain, Finland and the Netherlands.

To be clear: political and social agendas, urgent contexts, always told from the inside, with a fundamental principle, content, high stakes, inevitably, but also strong authored screenplays. We were definitively turning the page on "militant" cinema as we had known it, which had taught us the limitations of achieving what we wished to say at the expense of distinctive, cinematographic writing and without total engagement from the filmmaker, without addressing

---

* *South African Chronicles*, directed by 12 young filmmakers. Coordinated by A Van In and JL Portron, edited by Aurélie Ricard and produced as an extension of the work of the Varan Workshop in Johannesburg.

the essential question of the relationship between the filmmaker and the history he or she is addressing.

The environment I've described above had shifted by the end of the century. What revolutionised the field of documentary in the days of the "Arte-ZDF-Channel 4" gang (the Garrel, Stein and Fountain era, to name but a few) was very specifically the decision to bring films to the viewer, to feed the desire for films and to provide the means for them to exist, to privilege the authors, to drive creativity within economic constraints, and to do so by entrusting this role to independents who clearly shared this goal. We were part of it and had the chance to accompany the directors: a golden age.

And our reward is within reach, a new generation of creators, strong works and the success of the genre on air. Ambitious documentaries, non-standard lengths and formats that are up against the grid of the mainstream. A group of inventors who influence the entire landscape of cinematographic and audio-visual creation: Channel 4 shakes up the BBC, Arte shifts the boundaries of France 3, France 5 emerges, ZDF reinvents young German cinema. Foreign channels support the movement: Rai 3, TSR, which has a more journalistic tradition diversifies its commitments, Yle in Finland takes part in almost all ventures, and many others. The influence of what is in part the appearance of a second-generation in television shakes a whole landscape that has become increasingly formulaic, *caught up in large integrated companies. Since it

---

* There is much to be said about the undermining of the major public systems, deemed too heavy and unmanageable, which is a prelude to privatisation on the one hand and to the appearance of these new so-called "second generation" channels which no longer produce creative work in house. This movement, accompanied by the European institutions, gave rise to independent production.

does not favour creativity, it is destroying the areas of inventiveness and freedom that used to exist, such as the great BBC and ORTF (no nostalgia), where creators performed miracles. Another era.

And this movement stealthily changes the game. The success of these works run up against schedules which progressively stifle the exceptional. The same question rears its head again: how to safeguard the audience that has been won? The guardians of these schedules, their ratings in hand, become those who know what the public wants, what they need to see and hear, and everything is reversed. A documentary commissioning editor decides that it is vital to make a series about love at the age of twenty. He contacts a producer who is only too happy to receive this great suggestion, and the producer calls an author, who is totally involved in other things but is not going to object given the chance of getting paid work. We are no longer anchored to an author's deep-rooted desire to bring his/her work to an audience. Instead, he/ she is asked to reappropriate a story that is not his/ her own and respond to the thoughts of someone who has the means to produce and who 'knows' what the audience wants. The first years of this century were marked by this shift, admittedly more subtle and gradual than described here, and unsurprisingly the genre was impoverished to make way for accessible norms that were easy-to-read. Raymond Chandler wrote in a letter to Charles Morton in 1950, primarily referring to television, "There you are, watching the bubbles of the primeval ooze. You don't have to concentrate…You don't miss your brain because you don't need it. Your heart and liver and lungs continue to function normally… You are in the poor man's nirvana."* An unanticipated exercise in amnesia. What caused the original success is simply forgotten: a strong renaissance of creativity, especially in documentary, foundational genre for the whole of cinema.

The most spectacular story of amnesia is undoubtedly the Channel 4 experience in the UK. A very British story, somewhat incongruous, of a public channel, financed through the advertising revenues of other private channels, with the sole directive of engaging freely in all the areas neglected by the existing channels, addressing all minorities, exploring the margins, distant languages and forgotten territories. An era teeming with creation in all directions. Together we gave birth to the first Papua New Guinean feature film *Tinpis Run*,† to the South African Chronicles, we travelled through Africa, Palestine and Latin America.

At the end of fifteen years of freedom, an extraordinary lesson in the value of audacity, the channel achieves twelve percent of the audience, a level necessary to allow the channel to finance itself independently through advertising. And then, unexpectedly, everything falls apart. The team that had led Channel 4 to this formidable audience result was replaced by a new one who came up with their own formula, 'sex, drugs and video', with the aim of maintaining this audience. No more subtitles allowed, reversion to the national and in a unitary language,

---

* Raymond Chandler, *Selected Letters* (ed. Frank MacShane) (Columbia University Press, 1981), 241.
† *Tinpis Run* (1991), directed by Pengau Nengo with a team entirely from Papua New Guinea. Resulting from the work of Ateliers Varan and an exceptional man Severin Blanchet, victim of an attack in Kabul in 2003. Production JBA Production, Arte, Channel 4, Skul Bilong Wokin Piksa.

English. The erasure, pure and simple, of what was the greatness of this channel. Amnesia.[*]

A young Cambodian filmmaker

Eckart Stein wrote to me from Mainz — a handwritten letter of the time — and recommended a young Cambodian filmmaker whom no-one in France wanted to work with. I call him and he sends me a three-hundred-page draft. It contains everything, the history of his country, his terrifying journey the country during the Khmer Rouge terror, ending up miraculously in a refugee camp on the Thai border, Site 2.

The document does not reach me through the anonymous daily courier (email didn't exist then) but through a letter of introduction from a friend, an established connection. First and foremost there's a script, essential to read before speaking. I drown in its chaos but it's impossible not to meet this young filmmaker. We talk for about twenty hours over three days. We argue: the confrontation between the young Buddhist with a touch of René Char and the old/young Marxist that I was. But a project sprang up as a result.

If the potential of a cinematic event lies in the strength of the relationship between the filmmaker and his project this young man exemplifies it disproportionately. Everything proves exceptional — his history, his adolescent experience, his brief history in France, his poetry, his intelligence — and his personality is also out of the ordinary. Whatever the difficulties to be overcome, it is obvious that a film must be made.

---

[*] The original Channel 4 experience owes much to the visionary Jeremy Isaacs, who was in charge from 1982 until 1993.

The decision to produce

Therein lies the basis of what informs a decision to produce. A story, a filmmaker, an insider view, an overwhelming filmmaker-subject relationship and, in addition to the length of time it has taken to find this story, a strong creator, one who is guaranteed to surprise us and from whom we will never stop learning. To complete these criteria: a person we can trust to set out with on the long journey necessary for a film to be born.

As always, there are countless adventures. Rithy maintains an epistolary relationship with the refugee camp, and to return is to fulfil a promise, essential to himself but also inspired by the terror rooted in his history. At the time I only grasped fragments of it, but even then with incredulity, because the story is so intensely cruel. We will go on to make several films together but I had to wait for the publication and reading of his immense 2011 book *The Elimination*, written with Christophe Bataille, to understand the full dimension of the story. On the train to Geneva, where we are headed to plead our case, I discover that he has written the entire film scene by scene and in the greatest detail in order to confront his fear. "You do realise that in reality it will be completely different, so why are you doing this?" "I know," he replies, "but it's the only way I've found to exorcise my fear of returning to the camp."

We spend weeks in Bangkok, moving from embassy to embassy to find support but mostly waiting for a film permit to come through. The Thai military are suspicious about the entry of a European film crew led by a young Cambodian who speaks the language and is a former occupant of the camp where the Rangers continue to carry out their daily abuse. From our small hotel we write letters to the military authorities asking for permission. Or rather, *I* write them. Rithy cannot bear to have a hand in these "pleas to the bastards," and we wait, for days and weeks. Europe supports us: Arte, ZDF and Channel 4, the original trio. They have even formed themselves into a sort of club that they call *Quantum*, needing to stick together in the face of the threats that weigh in on these rare spaces of creativity. But what good is this support without permission to enter the camp? The situation is proving absurd. A green light finally reaches us. Permission for three days, strictly supervised. Once in the camp, Rithy will manage to stay there with his team for more than three weeks through all sorts of tricks and ploys. In the birth of a film the part played by tenacity, by obstinacy and relentless work, alongside the vision and talent, will always be a determining factor. A magnificent team too, Bouquin and Brisson, unflagging accomplices in the adventure. This is how his first, and magnificent first, feature-length documentary, *Site 2*, comes into being.

Iran, the meeting

Yalda is the culmination of six years' work with a film-maker whose first film we produced and supported, after an initial meeting twelve years ago. Marianne recalls: "Massoud couldn't bear to be the last in line during these improbable exercises in 'pitching' at one of the workshops that support world cinema. So he left the room. After he had left, the audience had to wait for him to come back, to make his way down, without hurrying, from the back of the Rai auditorium, and to take to the podium to tell his story." Marianne was impressed by his presentation and contact is established. This translates into further meetings, the first concrete discussions, that founding moment in our profession.

It was a long and tortuous story. A disappointing collaboration with Iran but in the end a rather strong result, even if the film is uneven in many respects. It is a first film and lands in Cannes at the Directors' Fortnight followed by a release in France through a good distributor. A definite success.* The only problem is that the film is political and attacks the corruption of Ahmadinejad's regime head on. The French and international press pick it up, carried away, celebrate the filmmaker and the subject, and the Mullahs wait with bated breath. Massoud does not want to choose exile. He does not want to stay in France. His mother, his father, his friends are waiting for him and Iran is his country. Not for one moment does he think of joining the exiles' club: he would rather return and face the Revolutionary Guards.

After four years of trials, death threats and work embargos, our partner, the Iranian producer, a solid figure in the sector, finds himself blacklisted, almost obliged to shut up shop, and forced to reimburse the television company that had invested in the film. The film is totally banned in Iran but widely distributed behind the veil, something which does not help our author's case.

A long journey through the desert begins. Showing his resilience, Massoud writes a small book that is "published." First sign of a period of relaxation. He shoots a documentary and manages to travel to Europe to expedite the new project. A second sign of

---

* *A Respectable Family*, produced by JBA and Firoozei Films (2012), distributed by Pyramide.

relaxation. This paradox named Iran where ultimately, in the stifling atmosphere generated by the current "Islamic Republic," everything always seems to be possible.

To hang, or not to hang

They close our account three months before the shoot. It's a disaster. The film is supported by nineteen funding sources, mostly European, all of them enthusiastic about the project, of which three —Swiss, German and the Luxembourgish—are co-producers. From nineteen sources a little more than a million euros, a budget that makes our colleagues in the French film industry, whose budgets are four times larger than ours, smile with sympathetic condescension.[*]

The story Massoud imagines revolves around the law of retribution. In Iran, for those sentenced to death, only the victim's family can grant a pardon. This long-standing tradition is to be the subject of one of Iran's major television shows, *The Pleasure of Forgiveness*. Will the young murderess be pardoned after 90 minutes of the show, with reports, investigations, debates, poems, songs, publicity, millions of text messages and, above all, a confrontation on stage? To hang or not to hang?

Massoud takes inspiration from one of the weekly mass TV events that exist in his country under the evocative title of *Honeymoon*; a reality show broadcast during the month of Ramadan that tries to win forgiveness to get a few condemned people off death row by applying the law of retribution in their

---

[*] Average budget of French fiction films 4.9 million euros. Source CNC 2019.

favour. After China, Iran is now the world's leading executioner. Live confrontations between the accused and the victim's family are guaranteed to be a popular success.

Massoud draws on true stories about the destinies of young women sentenced to death which he has come across in his documentaries. The tortuous, linear story, a bit laborious at first, evolves. The time for his rehabilitation with the authorities is put to good use. We are fully engaged and, like all screenplays, it progresses and is refined. The work takes the usual time necessary to reach maturity, a little over three years.

Writing is a long journey. For Massoud, the path is punctuated by workshops and meetings that are always productive and that will obviously contribute to the development of the script. It is significant that in France, where the film originated, there is practically no support for this writing stage largely because the language of the film is not French. No CNC, no Procirep,* just Angoa† for a very modest sum. By chance Massoud has family ties in the North of France so we will qualify for modest but precious support from the Haut de France region.

On the basis of the first screenplay, Massoud is selected by the Groupe Ouest: the first plunge. Massoud, a great swimmer, immerses himself in the cold sea of northern Brittany—first responses, confrontations with analysts, "script doctors" as they are known. The exercise is always perilous, like any journey where different points of view are jostling around, sometimes

---

* PROCIREP, a company that collects and redistributes funds for the benefit of producers, to compensate for the piracy of works in France.
† ANGOA, a company that collects and redistributes funds to compensate producers for the piracy of works abroad.

judicious, relevant, sometimes totally inconsequential. This will be the experience throughout the whole journey because even if these contributions are not all valid, at the end of the road they all prove useful so long as the filmmaker remains firmly anchored in his story. Filmmakers who are more fragile, still finding their way, can find themselves destabilised by these parallel participants, especially when they pull the script unhelpfully towards their own vision, into their own mould. Massoud listens, sifts through and most importantly, between each stage, we meet again which gives us the opportunity to test the fruits of these encounters.

After Brittany, the project is selected by the Torino Film Lab, a more sophisticated machine structured through several stages. First, the project is discussed with experts as a result of which it then goes into a kind of competition with awards. Massoud's project goes on to win the two main prizes. Between the stages of Torino, the Fabrique des Cinémas du Monde in Cannes picks up the project, after a battle to convince this fine team that the project definitely needs its backing. We often find ourselves victims of a reaction which assumes, given our background and experience, that we do not need this type of support. Absurd. This resource from Cannes proves useful and delivers results. It's a well-established organisation welcoming both filmmaker and the producers (this is still exceptional), offering important introductions and on this occasion Switzerland and Lebanon climb aboard. Above all, for us this means having a filmmaker in France for a fortnight: two weeks of non- stop discussion, precious moments. Finally, in January, the Sundance Film Festival selects him for a week of writing in Utah. More advisors, more opinions from another planet, a seminar that Massoud finishes in style by winning the prize awarded at the end of these encounters.

Whilst the usefulness of these meetings can be variable, they give an international status to the project, to the author and to the screenplay which is emerging within this small world of cinema. These are essential stages in this long journey bringing together the community of all those who are going to allow this project to succeed. It is still difficult to sustain production through these stages, to find the funding that will allow the author to survive whilst also sustaining our own existence. These meetings can be costly but they can also contribute significantly to raising the finance, as in the case of Torino and Sundance.

Massoud writes in Farsi and at a point when the screenplay is sufficiently accomplished we decide to have it translated into French by a professional, an indispensable step in moving on to another level of collaboration. It's often the case that on the eve of the shoot there is hardly anything left of this translation. It's a long process and luckily we are working with a filmmaker who speaks French well. For whole periods he writes in Iran, alone, and then in our meetings in Paris we discover the major shifts, take up our discussions again and throw everything into question. Changes are translated into Farsi which he reads back to us and we write the French version. We are never authors as such, just a sounding board, a work support, sporadic remedy for the solitude of an author confronting his screenplay. By the end of this long collaboration, we know every inch of this screenplay, a level of engagement that is fundamental in building the intimate trust that will nourish the

entire production process. After the initial decision
to produce, it is this time of development, the time to
immerse oneself in the work of creation, that provides
the second critical bedrock for our profession.

Working with an author who speaks our language
is a privilege: to be able to dive into the text with
great precision, to be able to explain and confront
each other with all the nuance of words, to eliminate
ambiguities and to save time. On several occasions
we have been condemned to use English. Everything
becomes heavier, more complex, an infinite source of
misunderstandings, and in crisis situations—memories
of Palestine or South Africa come to mind—words
proved imprecise even when they were not, tragically,
lacking.

We reckon that we've arrived at a version that
all three of us consider suitable for circulation. The
narrative has been squeezed into the length of time
of the TV show. The film begins with the arrival of
the protagonists at the studio and ends ninety minutes
later with their separation. Everything is told while the
show is in progress, partly on set but largely behind
the scenes, the whole punctuated by essential news
bulletins that help to inform the viewer. The story
unravels, loses control, the producer and the presenter
do their utmost to keep the show on the road, the
public is on the edge of its seat. The programme
must succeed, especially as we are at the high point of
the season, the night of Yalda, the great Zoroastrian
feast which marks the longest night of the year, 21st
December.

Putting the screenplay into circulation

A screenplay in hand triggers the search for the funding necessary for the adventure. Another key stage: the moment when the project is deemed ready for release. It's a stage that is not always obvious to the filmmaker, sometimes even incomprehensible, but this is one of our functions, to be the intermediary between creativity and the financing of creativity. It's a responsibility to protect an impatient author, a responsibility to make the film happen, to succeed and thus to take the right decision at the right time. It's a responsibility that does not make us infallible because we are intermediaries, tasked with understanding the environment around us and experience shows that we cannot avoid the probability of errors in reading the situation in play.

Each film is a prototype, every experience is different and yet everything repeats itself. It's impossible to copy from models. There would be too many variables that break the rule. We do not reproduce, we produce. The reality on the ground at each stage remains unpredictable. It is impossible, for example, to programme for or to set up the perfect schedule. Between Maria de Medeiros' *April's Capitains*[*] and Raoul Peck's *Lumumba*,[†] the initial time allowed between the two films was manageable. But then dear Raoul becomes Minister of Culture in Haiti—two years' postponement. So Maria moves ahead of him. Even that is too predictable. Now

---

[*] Directed by Maria de Medeiros Produced by Jba Production, Arte Cinéma, Mutante Filmes (Port), Alia Film (Ital), Filmart (Esp) and France 2 Cinéma. 2000.

[†] Directed by Raoul Peck produced by Jba Production, Arte Cinéma, Rtbf, Entre Chien et Loup (Bel), Essential Filmproduktion (All), Velvet Film. 2000.

Maria gets engaged with another creation, precious in another way, that of being a mother. The year's gap is shattered, and these two films, meticulously scheduled so as not to coincide with each other and not to strain our modest structure, end up shooting at the same time, just a few weeks apart. Then, finally, they screen at the Cannes Film Festival two days apart, having both been selected.

Both films come in at more than four million euros per film, even with our usual economies. The battle to finance them is relentless. Each one is going to fall short of around 150,000 euros, not much in respect of our overall budget, but coming together it's a mortal blow for an organisation like ours. In addition to the regular losses accumulated by documentary production (you budget at 100%, you start production with 80%, and you end up spending 110% - it's always the same story), this loss leaves us facing bankruptcy in all its glory. Filing for bankruptcy, closing down, leaving debts right, left and centre, only to be reborn in a new company—that's the classic trajectory. However, we decide to carry on and it will take us more than five years to pay back our debts and after ten years we shrink the organisation from nine people to just the two of us today, Marianne and I, with the part-time support of an accountant. Ultimately, this allows an exceptional freedom through the lightness of our operation. In summary, this is our deliberate and unavoidable choice—to sustain a company in order to give birth to films, rather than producing films to keep an enterprise alive and in profit.

Each film represents an equation to be solved, the rules of which change each time. On one side there is a project with all its characteristics and on the other the solution to be found. If we understand the creative proposal well enough and have enough knowledge and experience to master the economics of production, we can assess whether the equation is resolvable or whether we risk leading a creator, and his or her dreams, to certain failure.

There have been times when we've committed to equations that are improbable on paper. To return to April's Captains: on the left of the equals sign a magnificent historical project, everything reconstructed, an international cast, thousands of extras and armoured vehicles, located in the centre of Lisbon, one great actress confirmed, but nonetheless it's still a first film. To the right of the equals sign the advice of any sensible professional that it's "impossible," that "this filmmaker should start by making short films, or even a more intimate, cheaper film, before making this one." And yet we will succeed, though only because of the director's extraordinary talent and energy.

We have also produced a mathematician capable of drawing up an equation whose terms contain the solution from the start, thus offering the remedy to cure his bulimia, his impatience. Merzak Allouache hates waiting. For *The Rooftops* (2013), he invents the perfect device to allow him to shoot this feature-length fiction film in eleven days, on a derisory budget of around three hundred thousand euros, something never done before, at least by us. It's a film of such originality and strength that it lands in competition in Venice. Five stories, on five terraces, in fact, five short films. It avoids the intractable problems of shooting in the streets of Algiers, uses a team of young technicians eager to learn from the master and available from dawn to dusk and it's secure in the comfort of these magical open-air locations with committed actresses and actors. A film that explores this other Algiers: the stories, the greatness, the misery, the violence of life on the terraces of this surprising city. But it's exceptional, at least for us. Merzak takes everyone by storm with his talent and solid experience. We had booked our plane tickets to Algiers in order to join him at the beginning of the third week and almost by chance the French sound engineer rings us, "When are you coming?" "On Sunday" I reply. "Oh well, no need. The shoot's over and we're busy celebrating."

Perfume from Tehran

They close our account and it's clear that producing a film without a bank account is almost impossible. The money is mostly in place and all our partners let us know that they are happy to work with us as lead producer* because in the three countries concerned, as in France, it has become difficult to work with Iran. Our banks are strict. They rule out direct or indirect transactions with this country. We recognise the music, which has already been played to us. The difficulty is organisational and political. After Trump's relaunch of the embargo, the fear of sanctions closes all doors to the banking institutions. It also has practical consequences as it imposes another restriction: no money transfers to this country. So we have to finance the Iranian part of the film, the shoot.

Everything takes place in a studio and on one set. We have been working with Massoud, for some time now, on the idea of going to shoot elsewhere—Lebanon, Romania, Greece—anticipating this complex mess and above all having bad memories

---

* In co-productions, the term 'lead producer' (producteur delegué) describes the producer who acquires the rights, signs off on contracts and has final responsibility for the film and its release.

of our collaboration with Iran on the previous film. But Massoud remains firm, "I will not shoot abroad. It would be a definitive way of being considered an 'enemy agent', and I don't want to lose the perfume of Tehran. Everything can be felt in a film, down to the smallest details, the accents, the extras. You know this." And yes, we know this. He's right, damn him, but filming in Iran is still a very delicate matter.

In the absence of a co-production agreement between France and Iran and given the lack of funding on the Iranian side (we'll come back to this), it is imperative that the production be classified as European, with all the constraints that this entails for an Iranian film shot in Iran. If not, the film cannot be financed. Our first objective is therefore to set up the production on the European side. In the absence of solid French partners, with the exception of the Breton fund (obtained as an extension of the writing workshop at the Groupe Ouest via a local producer who sought support from the Region) and one other straightforward and significant support from the Hauts de France region, we go back to those who had previously shown an interest in the project. First of all Switzerland, through a co-producer we met in Cannes during the Fabrique des Cinémas du Monde, co-producer of Massoud's first film. She likes the proposal and enthusiastically launches herself into the attack on her national and regional funds and Swiss television, and with success. In France, Arte is not interested in the project. It's hard to accept this, that this once unique partner for foreign language films has become an impregnable fortress. It feels worse because we have produced fifteen feature films with Arte France, all of which, without exception, were selected at Cannes, including seven first films. But this is the way with any competitive process. We then turn to Arte in Germany, to long-term friends.

This is the continuation of a story that began more than thirty years ago with the film by Rithy Panh, through Eckart Stein, the magician of this mythical department of ZDF, Das Kleine Fernsehspiel. It's a rare island of creativity attached to the realm of Germany's second public channel, which has survived thanks to the strength of their inventiveness and their audacity. Our partner is Doris, who started in this department some thirty years ago alongside Eckart. She reads, reacts quickly, asks all the questions arising from the project, likes it, and offers to recommend it to her department. The discussion widens, they work in a collective way. The decision-making process from Mainz to Strasbourg turns out to be tortuous, but in the end they commit. This is a significant step in the financing process, not in terms of the amount—which is not negligible—but in terms of the legitimacy it gives to the project. This decision opens the door to a German producer and everything becomes easier on the German side as soon as a channel commits itself.

It then becomes possible to submit the project to a fund dedicated to cooperation between France and Germany, a competitive fund which eventually supports us. France returns through a door left open on our eastern borders. On the strength of these commitments the German production wins the support of several regions, the *länder*, funds that are accompanied by obligations to spend in these territories, the management of which is delicate.

We fail with Arte France but also with the only French fund for this type of film, the Aide au Cinémas du Monde (ACM). The screenplay is twice selected for the plenary commission, the final decision stage, but then the project is twice rejected. This is also hard to bear. We can survive, but, crucially, what is at stake is the life of a filmmaker. Once again, this is the nature of all competitive funds but for us it is a close, fraternal, founding partner. Our entire production history has been underwritten by this type of support, which makes these latest judgements particularly painful.

Thirty years earlier, we were among the first to be supported by this fund, then called Fonds Sud, for the first feature film directed by a Papua New Guinean filmmaker, Pengau Nengo. It was a support that enabled us to give birth to the works of Rithy Panh, Raoul Peck, Ramadan Suleman, Teresa Villaverde, Massoud Bakhshi (for his first film), Merzak Allouache, Pablo Agüero, Fernando Guzzoni, Annemarie Jacir, Serguei Loznitsa… Of course, they may think "we've already funded you," but we know that each project is unique. Regardless of our record there is no easy way through, no priority given, and the members of the commission have the final word. In France we have practically no alternatives for this type of cinema.

I was a member of this fund for four years alongside people who were forceful in the defence of a certain type of cinema: Pierre Chevalier, Claire Denis, Alain Rozanes, Frédéric Mitterrand. This was well before Mitterand became Minister of Culture and decided in a very French flight of fancy to transform it from the aptly named Fonds Sud (South Cinema Fund) into a planetary fund, Aide aux Cinémas du Monde (Aid to World Cinemas), precipitating a lightning multiplication in the number of applicants for almost the same amount of money. You don't have to be a mathematician to predict the consequences: more applicants from all over the world so fewer are chosen. And this in an environment that is the same throughout Europe and the world, wherever such funds exist.

It is a bitter setback for the project, especially since France is the originating country and it hasn't followed through: a negative indication for our legitimacy with all future partners. So, after Switzerland and Germany, we set out to take on Luxembourg, which has created a fund inspired by our Aide aux Cinémas du Monde (ACM). To apply we need a local partner. We research the field, and after many failures finally manage to convince an Austrian-Luxembourg producer partnership that Massoud had met at the Mia Market in Rome. The application to this World Cinema Fund is dependent on an interview with the commissioners. Massoud accompanies us. He proves to be particularly convincing and we leave the meeting with the strong impression that we've won the battle. In fact, we soon learn that they have decided to back us, enthusiastically. A third partner is therefore in place. In the meantime, at Cannes we have met a Lebanese friend and partner, Georges S, wealthy and with a real passion for cinema, who likes the project, trusts us, and gets involved. The finance package is becoming clearer and with these commitments we submit the project to a major European fund, Eurimages,* which also decides to support us. A Belgian partner will be added a little later.

Now the absolute priority is to travel to Iran to find the dream partner without whom this film will be impossible. A long nightmare is in preparation.

---

* Eurimages is the cultural support fund of the Council of Europe. established in 1989

Memories of Palestine

Working with a country alongside women and men who suffer daily, who are marginalised, occupied and humiliated, is always a challenge. We were travelling by car with Annemarie in the north of what she calls historic Palestine, scouting for locations for her film, driving past clumps of prickly pear cactus flanked by tall cypresses, often surrounded by fields of olive trees, a sure sign of the sunken ruins of Palestinian villages emptied of their inhabitants, expelled to camps where many of them still live. The atmosphere is charged but warm and we are on our way back to Nazareth to meet the co-producer for the Palestinian side of the film, someone Annemarie dreams of working with: "He's been an activist from way back, a filmmaker and producer. He works a lot with Europe. You'll see, he's great."

It's obvious from the start he doesn't like us. He hates the fact that Annemarie is working with French people and sings from a hymn sheet we immediately recognise. He knows everything about everything, better than we do. He knows everyone in Europe, better than we do. He has access to all the funds, with better contacts than ours, and so on. Honestly, what are we doing here, trying to do what he can do so much better than we can? We have been living with this project for two years. We have translated successive versions of the screenplay and Annemarie trusts us. Our eyes meet.

That dinner remains a dreadful memory, a shame because the cuisine proves exceptional. Silence is interspersed with these bantering culinary exchanges. The atmosphere becomes charged and gently rises. I lose my temper. With age I have lost the tolerance necessary for this type of situation. Marianne is more patient. When the deserts are served I throw everything back in his face. Why should we bother to make the least concession to him? Annemarie takes a nose-dive but understands everything. Exit this co-producer. Nightmare number one.

The next producer, also proposed by our filmmaker, is the best in the business. He is experienced and has a team. It is based in Israel. They are so-called "Israeli Arabs," which is obviously an advantage especially since Annemarie has set the rules of the game from the start: "I will not work with Israelis. I don't want any funds, any aid, any Israeli company on board." In contrast to the first man, B, not a militant but a pragmatic technician, plays it modestly, low key. He agrees on practically everything, is attentive, professional. He has solutions, proposes figures. Only one question never gets answered, that of his fee. We insist, we come back to him. We want to make informed estimates taking everything into account, otherwise it is impossible to know how much to budget for the film. "It's not a problem. We can resolve that later," he repeats. It's of such concern that we invite him to Paris to press him further, to try and understand what's behind this refusal to clarify his status in the film. Nothing to be done. He remains vague and systematically sidesteps the issue. On his return he puts together the team and plays for time knowing that, with three weeks to go before the shoot, his hands will be free and we will be tied hand and foot. We know this too, and it is precisely what happens.

We return to Ramallah a little more than three weeks before the shoot. Unlike on previous visits he doesn't come to welcome us, arriving at the meeting point two hours late. He speaks to us, that is he speaks to me. He never looks Marianne in the eye, the eyes of a woman, a behaviour we've come across in other similar situations, not only in the Arab world. So he tells me in summary, "You are here in my house. This is my land, my country, my expertise, you know the rates. From now on I am the producer in charge and this is my price. Send the money, I'll see to the rest." Classic. We saw it coming, we expected it but his manner is particularly brutal. We quietly retort, without the slightest hesitation, that he will not make the film. We are absolutely determined in the face of such a situation, one we know well. There's no need for consultation, we're absolutely clear. A violent meltdown ensues. He can't believe us. He thinks we're bluffing and that we'll call him back within hours. Two days of crisis meetings to establish who in his team will stick by him and who will decide to make the film without him. We're told he is crying in the next office. There's no way we're going to give in. We'd rather postpone the film than entrust it to someone in this position. The atmosphere is icy in these inauspicious offices. In Ramallah there is practically no central heating, severe cold is so rare. It must be three or four degrees outside, with a scattering of snow on the dusty ground. However, since taking our decision we have the unconditional support of the filmmaker. Once again, she has understood. She knows where her interest lies—with the interest of the film. Nightmare number two.

At the end of these three days, we find solutions without him, and the film is made on schedule. It will finish in Cannes, in the official selection, a few months later.

Tehran, first

Iran is a large country, modern and beyond question full of contrasts and contradictions. Tehran, 22 million inhabitants and almost as many cars, with many more Peugeots and Renaults than in Paris. The pollution is oppressive, the city suffocating, the traffic an indescribable chaos: think Naples compared to Switzerland. The only place in the world where we have seen worse is in Lagos. You can walk in safety in this city everywhere, day and night. There's just one deadly experience: the acrobatic exertion of the pedestrian in his attempt to cross the main roads.

Massoud, whose reputation is incendiary, moves towards T, a historic producer, well connected to the powers who can grant a film permit. We understand the rationale, but we know absolutely nothing about this partner and don't yet understand the extent of the difficulties that lie ahead. We make contact and begin the first steps of negotiation. The business turns out to be complicated and we discover quite definitely that we will not find funding on the Iranian side due to the general crisis, the ongoing embargo (particularly affecting the film sector though it continues to produce more than a hundred films per year) but also because of Massoud's sulphurous impact on the terrain. The Iranian part of the project must therefore be financed entirely with European money.

And here we come up against a recurring scenario. How to find an Iranian producer who will undertake a film by an Iranian filmmaker in Iran when he is not the producer, when he must work with a script and finance package that are completely locked, with European money to boot and powerful patrons from elsewhere? In terms of self-interest it's unthinkable. There's also the burden, a classic "overhead" associated with the seductive scent of foreign money. We are seen as rich and prosperous, almost American, while in fact we are corseted into a tight budget, bound by all kinds of obligations and far from closing the circle. It's still a film in Farsi, by a virtually unknown filmmaker and without a cast. There is a lot of love and passion for Iranian cinema but very little money.

And this Iranian producer, just to make things easier, hasn't produced for years and what's more, he has great difficulty in getting around. He suffers, Massoud tells us, from a major disability. The contacts get bogged down, we don't hold all the cards, and the three-month authorisation granted to the film expires. We discover with surprise, and this is a recurring theme with our dear director, that he assumes the ultra-short duration of the film permit, six months, will force us to shake up the schedule even when absolutely nothing is in place.

"Massoud, we will shoot when the money is in place. We cannot take the risk of not paying you, the crew, for the film in general, of not finishing, of not delivering. And you know us well by now: no personal fortunes and after more than a hundred films, always broke, with two to three months in play. In short, we live on the edge and you know it. There is no question of committing to production before we've consolidated the funding and found all the partners." As time passes it creates tension, a weariness. Massoud has been working on this script for almost four years. The urgency now is to shoot, as soon as possible. A legitimate aim.

Going into production

Another key moment in this business is the decision to go into production. The finance must be in place before launching the adventure, without hidden costs (some production managers do this well, and the costs generally disappear at the time of post) while guaranteeing payment for the filmmaker, the crew, the suppliers, etc. This is a particularly delicate and complex issue as the decision-making factors are rarely in sync: season, availability of actors, key technicians, postponement of other commissions, delays in those engagements, disappearance of co-producers. Everything is in place, almost in shape, the boat is filling up. We may be far from resolving everything but we can no longer go back. We are already too far out to sea. The beauty in that idea, the one where we leave when everything is ready and the financing is all in place. It's an idea grandly and confidently affirmed in all the seminars, one which almost always flies off into space. And here we are, already embarked, like tightrope walkers.

With projects taken on from the start, very often with the beginnings of a screenplay, it's taking longer and longer. Less and less money, fierce competition, a real rush to find the funds that finance the type of cinema we are trying to defend. There's been an erosion of curiosity about the rest of the world, a comfortable retreat to the "domestic" as the Anglo-Saxons say, an erosion of audiences resulting from these "mainstream" policies, and unquestionably a change in the history of how we look at and consume images, sounds and music. Such fundamental shifts, but we are so busy with our noses to the grindstone that we live in reaction to such phenomena rather than making a serious analysis of these mutations. And the world remains vast and the pace of change takes many different forms. To put it simply, the competition is so fierce today that there is no choice but to raise the stakes higher.

It took us seven years to bring to life Pablo Agüero's *Eva Doesn't Sleep.*[*] An interminable writing process, though essential without the slightest doubt: almost ten treatments to resolve the insoluble problems of the story's structure and numerous versions of the screenplay. Finally, recognition: winning the prestigious Grand Prix du Scénario in France (for an Argentinean), the screenplay selected and broadcast by France Culture, read in front of an audience of eight hundred spectators in Angers by Jeanne Moreau, with a gravelly voice and passionate, roguish energy. The mischief of this immense actress pointing out Eva Perón's head lice, so close to the audience and with the "first lady" of François Holland's era sitting in the front row.

The film is very modestly budgeted at a little over two million. Enthusiastic partners scatter us with all sorts of promises and then withdraw them one after another. Granted, this is only the second feature film by a young, little-known Argentine filmmaker (the first, *Salamandra*, was only selected for the Directors' Fortnight). A film in Spanish, with an incomplete cast (Gaël Garcia Bernal and Denis Lavant) and an unusual story of the absurd wandering of Eva Perón's remains over a period of twenty-five years. "Ultimately a bit morbid for our public," one of the major subscription channels would tell us. At the end of a seven-year struggle, we had finally and painstakingly collected

---

[*] *Eva Doesn't Sleep* by Pablo Aguero, 2015, produced by JBA production and Haddock Films (Argentina)

a little less than 800,000 euros. During a beautiful month of August we had this discussion, delicate, bitter and cruel, with the aim of deciding whether to shoot with what we had or to let it fall apart for good. Pablo, exhausted, weary, like all of us, bounces back and with an intelligence matured over the years, finds artistic and technical solutions enabling him to go on to make, finally, a beautiful film.

The rare pearl

On the Iranian side, we are back to square one, with the first film permit expired and a producer no longer willing but still in charge of the project. And this producer has influence. The second chapter begins. This first producer throws in the towel and offers us the pearl of Iranian production, a woman, F, who has hardly any experience of film production with foreigners but who has a solid reputation, at least as far as we are able to assess at a distance. Massoud is delighted, pleased that there is finally a producer waiting for us in Tehran. Over the past few months we have watched a large number of Iranian films, scrutinised the credits, collected names, and tried to reconstruct the way forward, making proposals to Massoud.

And now a nagging feeling deeply instilled in us by Massoud, whom we love, is confirmed. The Iranians are not straightforward. In spite of the danger of generalising, we speak from experience in saying that they are masters of confusion, fanatics for negotiation, a veritable art form, systematically deploying forgetfulness and lies as a technique to advance in the direction that suits them. (Is this unique to the Iranians, I ask myself as I write these lines?). There is always a reason, whether political—often political since that works best—or technical or professional. "You won't understand, but this is Iran." Or they simply claim dishonesty, inefficiency, a lack of professionalism, or use even more surprising arguments like "They don't live in Tehran," or they just invent rules which turn out not to exist, such as "You have to have produced at least three feature films," etc… It will take us three years to understand how this works. The most important thing is not the lie but the cover up, the re-assertion of the truth as if was always obvious: "Don't you remember? That's exactly what I told you the first time."

And so, in short, F would be the pearl, the producer we had to have. And we, naïve for thirty-three years, believe it. At least we hope it will work out, and we get in touch. We WhatsApp. Everything goes well and we organise a first trip to Tehran with the aim of negotiating and signing with a partner who will take charge of the film in Iran.

What a great profession we're in, off to discover Persia, one of the cradles of civilisation with archaeological treasures unique to the world. We end up spending four days in offices, and we do this on every subsequent trip (we go to Iran eight times in two years): hotel, office, traffic jams, office, traffic jams, hotel.

Let's talk about the hotel. F has put us up "near the office." We're not choosy; it's a cheap film, but this is indescribable kitsch with sticky carpets, on a crossroads that could not be more noisy, above a packed avenue overshadowed by an urban motorway. Yes, we do have trouble coming to terms with it. It reminds me of negotiations at the *Boutiques Obscures*[*]

---

[*] Office of the Italian Communist Party Headquarters in Rome.

in Rome in the 1980s. They always used to put me up in the hotel located "nearby," half-way up an interminable hill, where buses and trucks would change into second gear, making hideous grinding noises, to finish the climb. Not a minute of sleep. I still suspect it was a deliberate ruse, because the next day I would collapse, exhausted, in their offices.

From the moment of arrival at the airport, Marianne wears a headscarf from breakfast onwards. Her arms and legs are covered to the wrists and ankles, but at least it is April and the temperature is still pleasant.

F, in her sixties, is a stout, lively woman, soberly yet firmly veiled, dressed in black and wearing a heavy set of keys as her only adornment. We are instantly in the presence of power. This woman, seated in her vast office, reigns over a small world of women who run things smoothly. The presence of her husband, reputedly a powerful figure in the Iranian film industry (he reigns from an office on the upper floor), lingers in the background. She welcomes us warmly and engages in quasi-formal preliminaries, steeped in trays of sweets, pistachios, almonds and dry cakes. We explain our complex production structure, with all its partners and their obligations on all sides, and finally offer her a role to suit her level of engagement, whether as co-producer, if she can find funding, or as executive producer, if she cannot. And here time gets swallowed up in the Persian carpet. F's technique is to change the subject all the time, never to answer a question until the very end. We exchange looks and patiently come back to the subject, there where it last lapsed. And then comes mealtime. This is going to last for four interminable days, four days where F is going to feed us: a fundamental element of protocol which delivers our gentle and inevitable dependence. The food arrives in cardboard boxes and it's almost always the same thing. Over the following visits it will always be the same thing: rice, rice, rice, kebabs, chicken.

Then the discussion starts again. We keep pressing her to get a hint of an answer to our initial question. What was mentioned earlier about the impossible 'Iranian producer' strikes here in a surprising way. "I'm interested in this film, I want to make it. I don't understand why you're bothering with all these partners, all these complications. Give me 300,000 euros, go home quietly and I'll make the whole film for you, right down to the subtitled DCP." Back to square one. We take the blow. It's all the more surprising since she doesn't want to talk about the film, the screenplay, the filmmaker's previous work, of which she even presumes to say, with a shrug, "I haven't seen it." Translation: any person in a position of power in Iranian cinema should not have "seen" this banned and censored film. So what does she want? It will take us four days to figure it out, a little longer because the definitive, straight answer will only arrive in Paris, two weeks later.

For now, it's a deal. The package turns out to be good, as we say in this business. The filmmaker is promising and there is European money. We go through all the possible production models, co-producer with a substantial investment, then silence. She disappears to Shiraz for a whole day and leaves us to stew in our shabby hotel.

We grumble, speculate and think we've reached a dead end, that nothing will come of this meeting. Finally, we can't take it anymore. The desire to make a film with this woman evaporates. It's better to postpone, to change country, but above all not to commit ourselves in this way. Massoud doesn't understand the situation. The film is at the point of breakdown again. Finally, she reappears and says that she is willing to take on the executive production and that the cost of the Iranian part must now be calculated. Discussions ensue on the subject. Our stay overruns along with our patience. She puts us in the hands of a nice, power-less, worldly boy and two weeks later we receive a budget for the shoot, just the Iranian part: it is equal to the entire budget for the film, four times the cost presented on the first day for the full production of the film, including delivery of the DCP. Elegant. First visit.

Once a bank closes an account for such a clear reason, it remains complicated, to say the least, to go looking for others. All doors close as soon as we explain the situation. "Your bank is right, the same applies for us." Without a bank account, no film. It's mid-June and the shoot is still scheduled for mid-September. A disaster. A marathon begins. We explore the world of small private banks, including those tasked with trading with Iran. There are two of them, and we go back to old banker friends in the hope of support, of finding a business that would understand and commit. Our absurd situation reaches its peak. Nine-teen sources of finance have been offered, often with passion and enthusiasm, most of them institutional or quasi-institutional: Arte, the national film institutions of France, Germany, Switzerland and Luxembourg, distributors, agents, Iranian cinema. All these have expressed their support but not one bank is willing to accompany us on the adventure.

The financing of this film remains a long ordeal, not to mention the funding for development, which is totally non-existent for this type of project. These are long, complex financial arrangements, full of additional constraints and obligations. The challenge lies in respecting them while protecting the filmmaker and the film as much as possible. Co- production, unavoidable to gather a million euros for this type of project, is definitely a nightmare.

It is always an epic journey. We have produced one hundred and fourteen films, forty-two feature films, always in co-production, half of them first works and mainly as the initiators, the lead producer. We do not like to co-produce as a minority partner. Occasionally we have done so and almost always regretted it, even if some fine films have resulted. We don't like losing control at the moment when the film and the filmmaker most needs to be protected: when a film needs two more weeks of editing and the main producer declares "the edit is closed, I have no more money", or at the decisive moments when choosing an editor, a cinematographer, an actress, a mixer, a mixing studio, when this is 'imposed' against the wishes of the filmmaker due to production constraints. Ultimately, in our experience, with rare exceptions, co-production represents a long succession of bitter, painful failures. The films certainly reach completion: twenty-one go to Cannes, eight to Venice, four to San Sebastian, two to Berlin, two to Locarno and one to Sundance. But at what cost?

Tsai Ming-Liang

Our most wonderful experience in the management of limitations is the experience we had the opportunity to share with Tsai-Ming Liang, the renowned Malaysian filmmaker, Taiwanese by adoption. Henri Loyrette, then the head of the Louvre, decided to allow in film: a few of the living amongst the sublime dead who haunt the galleries and those kilometres of space which block the light between the picture rails and the windows. And in the first instance he sought out this rare filmmaker, an act of total and magnificent audacity, and invited him to come and immerse himself in this temple of culture (nicknamed by Ming-Liang "the dragon") and to use it as a location for a film. There were no institutional obligations except the requirement to shoot part of the project in the museum. A sort of golden trap for a profoundly free creator: the scent of a 'commission' in a world that is the antithesis of his life, his culture and his history. But, like all the greatest, he is searching, obstinate, lucid, modest, free, joyful. Where it gets complicated is in the process of production. Tsai Ming-Liang's works, renowned the world over, remain little-known by the public. Because of this he shoots with modest means, with budgets that rarely exceed one million. But the Louvre's adventure will be expensive. We are in Paris, in complex working conditions, with known actors.

Faced with this problem, the Louvre calls us to help them solve this difficult equation: how to produce a Tsai Ming-Liang for three and a half million while avoiding all the predators, and everything that could obstruct the creative process due to the range of obligations imposed by this type of budget. "Why are you calling us?" "Because this is precisely what you know how to do, even if this filmmaker is not your cup of tea." We are taken aback. It is always surprising, if not hurtful, to realise how we are seen by others. "He is undoubtedly one of the filmmakers we most admire, one of the most important today." Tsai Ming-Liang's films are unforgettable—*The River*, *Vive l'Amour*, *Goodbye Dragon Inn* and so many others—and we respond without hesitation: "We are absolutely up for this venture."

We go on to make two films with him, surprised by his constant demand for discussion, for advice. We are prepared, this first time, to simply accompany and protect a master. But as the days (and nights) go by, we discover his solitude, his need of consultation, his doubts. When we travel to Taiwan, we learn just how alone he is, alone because he is surrounded by "disciples" caught in silent admiration for the master. We keep asking questions about different aspects of the film in the making. He stops, takes his time and finally almost always answers "I don't know." We can't help hearing an echo: the certainties of younger filmmakers who, without hesitation, always come up with the answer.

Lesson. That eternal debate around intuition, an essential space in the creative process but one which it is always productive to clarify. Debate around this "I feel it," which often simply masks uncertainty. We ask questions, a process that is essential to elucidate what this famous intuition hides. And during this clarification the vision sharpens and, above all, the filmmaker discovers a release that opens up new spaces for creation. With Ming-Liang, we explore his intuitions and each time obstacles and milestones are overcome. Let's be clear, he remains the absolute master. We try to be there for him when the need arises. Endless discussions, even though he doesn't speak a word of French or English, made possible thanks to the Franco-Taiwanese co-producer,[*] a true guardian angel, capable of reproducing these fluid exchanges with amazing skill and agility. Ming-Liang is a director who turns out

---

[*] Vincent Wang, co-producer, first assistant during *Face*.

to be an exceptional cook, and this is not by chance: he's used to feeding his crew on his shoots in Taipei. This proves an impossible task—a slight disappointment in Ming-Liang's eyes—in the face of the sixty or so people busy on the set of *Face*. Lots of love all the time. He discovers that French people kiss in the morning at the beginning of the shoot and sometimes also at the end of the working day. So he takes this on and commits to kissing everyone: the technical team, the actresses, the actors. In the culinary field, he finally makes up for lost opportunities by cooking during the entire edit process. He leaves the editing room in good time to do the shopping and returns in the morning with his plastic bags containing dishes of great delicacy.

Then comes the stage of production approval by the CNC, Centre du Cinema, called the agreement. In the middle of all the happiness, one of the greatest difficulties in this universe of rules, points, committees of approval, and European qualifiers is to protect Tsai Min-Liang from it. The approval is rejected by the CNC, two weeks before the shoot, and it turns out we are to blame for insisting on our Taiwanese director of photography. Without approval, there will be no film, because eighty percent of the financing will collapse. We are ready to shoot, everything is in place. We submit a new application to the commission, but at the same time—total madness—we launch into the shoot. A director of the CNC just happens to be strolling through the gardens of the Louvre with her family one day and comes across a small sign hanging on a gate blocking her access to part of the park. To her astonishment, she discovers that a film is in production for which her institution has refused approval, only the week before. The basic problem—

everyone agrees that this film should happen—is inflexibility, sometimes legitimate, of the professional organisations represented by the production committees. But this kind of minor ordeal is a reminder of the fragility of the edifice on which we constantly depend. It's one of the small miracles of this profession that, in the overwhelming majority of cases, we reach the shoot, in vessels of impossible risk, yet we always get through. This powerful film ends up in Competition at Cannes.

And we will have the pleasure of co-producing another film by this director, *Stray Dogs*, which will win the Grand Prix du Jury in Venice in 2013 and of which our dear Isabelle Régnier will write in her review in Le Monde: "Two stray dogs, two blocks of solitude in ruins that leave the viewer stunned. It's as if they've just seen the last shot of the last film in the history of cinema, in which the silhouettes of the last man and woman in the world vanish into thin air."* Her words make you seriously ask yourself whether we shouldn't just have left it at that.

Co-production is a nightmare

There are many good reasons for this. A co-producer who has not initiated the project, has not developed it, has virtually no engagement with the filmmaker. Why would he or she commit to the venture? Understanding why a co-producer decides to come in on a film is probably the most significant factor in managing any future relationship. Likewise, going to meet him/her where he/she lives and works, because

---

* "Deux chiens errants, deux blocs de solitudes en ruines qui laisse le spectateur terrassé. Comme s'il venait de voir le dernier plan du dernier film de l'histoire du cinéma où s'évanouissaient les silhouettes du dernier homme et de la dernière femme de l'humanité."

most of the time what's essential to know is revealed there. Once in Argentina, we land in brightly lit, landscaped offices where a dozen young women work in silence behind their computers, to be directed into a plush office where the man, the producer, reigns. We know with absolute certainty that we are not at home.

Why does a producer get involved? The answers are numerous. There's the hierarchy of experience and skill. A young producer might find it worthwhile to enter a strong project that genuinely interests him or her and which—through the analysis he/she makes of the journey ahead—could take him/her far afield, on coloured carpets: an opportunity to travel with people of experience and an opportunity to learn. There's the producer who may simply base his/her rationale on largely financial grounds. The project is good, the business is up and running: "I co-produce, I take little risk, my name is on the poster, I appear on stage, I have the film in my filmography as a producer and my fee is assured." This is because the representative at the end of the chain, responsible for delivery, is the only one who risks not being paid. Another type is an old friend who enters the dance to do us a favour, in solidarity, but who has been out of production for some time or who is over-committed already to his/her own projects. Usually most solid producers prefer not to co-produce as minority partners. They produce their own films, like we do. Another type is the one invited in from the country where we are going to shoot, and this one, an unavoidable player, as we have already described, finds him/herself in an untenable position both for him/herself and consequently for us.

We have produced films in more than thirty countries, from Cambodia to South Africa, from Argentina to Chile, from Belgium to Portugal, and sometimes

the deadlock has been such that we have been forced
to create our own company on the spot—in Portugal
and South Africa for example. Another drawback,
because you can't manage a company in the long term
from a distance and in both cases the main challenge
was to manage the company's closure while limiting
the damage. It took more than eight years to get rid
of the Portuguese company, created to produce Maria
de Medeiros' *April's Captains* and Teresa Villaverde's
Os Mutantes. And all of this was due to a series of
tedious battles to recover the VAT that the tax authorities had decided not to refund. We persisted, got into
debt, were far too far from the terrain of the film, and
finally gave up.

The experience of co-production reproduces
similar scenarios: incompetence, more often a lack of
commitment, leaving us obliged to compensate, to do
the work of others, even to train others. We are also
obliged to absorb the disappearances, which are very
common. They can be of varying duration and happen
for many reasons. Sometimes the co-producer has
taken on other films and this one is not his own, or "It
no longer answers my priorities." It happens repeat-
edly and without any notification, not by email, nor
phone, nor, nor… Response to emails has proved to
be a fundamental way of gauging the future of a relationship, of what lies ahead. Then the horror of financial negotiations which bear no relation to the film's
budget, its simple balance sheet, its coherence. The
absence, the resistance, the lack of transparency in the
face of aligning obligations between countries where
rules are clear, restrictive and, it's true, often contradictory. And as we are the first and the last in the chain,
we are obliged to be accountable to everyone. We run
and run—chasing film accounts, documentation from

the overseeing authorities. This is never-ending. There is no other option, as our co-producer, distant and elsewhere, has already moved on.

There is also the one (it happens frequently) who tells us, like B in Palestine, "You are not working in your home country. You cannot possibly understand. Just send the money and we will do the rest." It reminds me of the meeting we had with one of our co-producers with a lawyer in Johannesburg. It was for an earlier film, but nicely sums up the situation. The meeting takes place in the car park of one of these wealthy villas in the northern districts. The producer gets out of a gleaming, metallic blue, German sedan. "Jo, did you win the lottery?" "No. Always the same rule when I start a film: car first!"

We hate being in the dark, not being able to learn from these countries, not being able to predict what's going to happen, working without certainty that the small amount of money raised will go towards the film, and only the film. The arrival of a film production wherever, especially in countries with fragile economies but in others too, is always a boon. Only by taking the plunge, learning and understanding along the way, can you be sure that the rands, tomans, pesos, shekels, etc., will actually go into the creation of the film.

But worst of all are the egos. This profession generates egos which are out of the ordinary, starting with our own, and very often, to guarantee its existence, the ego becomes inversely proportional to the importance of its position in the production. An ego that thrives whether by disappearing so as to be desired or, more generally, by multiplying problems in order to exist, dragging them out, not to mention insisting on a hierarchy that bears no relation to the size of the companies involved. Trainees, assistants, secretaries, deputies... It's surprising, given there are just two of us doing everything, and we do not always understand these excessive teams, not least from the economic point of view. We don't talk directly to the co-producer but end up talking to the trainee who treats us as his equal. This is perfectly normal.

Egos can lead to a bloodbath at the time of negotiating credits if, from experience, we don't meticulously regulate this issue in the contracts. And the ultimate round takes place in the jostling when the time comes to walk the red carpet, pushing vigorously to get actresses, actors, director, producers to the centre of the photo. Here we speak of actual, specific and repeated experiences. Obviously, this does not do justice to the exceptions. These producers will easily recognise themselves but it is important to pay tribute to them for having transformed the nightmare into a pleasure, albeit this remains a rather rare experience. To be fair, these ego problems are mainly "lad" problems, aggravated when they are obliged to deal with a woman who is more competent than they are.

Co-producing is not just a nightmare in terms of setting up these hordes of co-producers and partners. It is also a technical exercise that requires real dexterity. Eight co-producing countries and nineteen sources of funding for Annemarie Jacir's first film *Salt of this Sea*, all for a little over a million euros. A real case study. Absurd, delirious, insane, our friends exclaim. Five countries for our Chilean friend for half a million. Twenty-one sources of funding for Raoul Peck's Lumumba and almost as many for Maria de Medeiros' April's Captains, with five countries on board. It is exceptional, but there have been examples where we have only brought in three countries. This is the price we have to pay for these films to exist. We have hardly any choice, let alone the time it takes to organise all these funds, to meet all the often excessive requirements and the effort to harmonise the often contradictory regulations.

Even between European countries the rules are incompatible and often absurd. The smallest co-producer country requires the certification of everyone else's accounts to validate its own. This is a snake with a sting in its tail: each co-producer waits for the others before they can act. The Spanish budgets include theatrical release costs which is not allowed in France. Contingencies are not allowed in Germany so they are disguised in each item which makes things more complex when it comes to establishing the actual budget. There's no real harmonisation of rights with the Anglo-Saxon world, a world upside down. Between the countries of Europe, Italy stubbornly continues to ask for rights in perpetuity (poor Beaumarchais[*] turns in his grave). The producer's salary is calculated as a percentage of expenditure in Belgium. Germany and Switzerland require their own contribution to the budget, a fictitious amount which they will not invest and which distorts everything. There's no budget sheet, no formula, no identical chart of accounts. The final delivery of accounts is a small miracle, where the imperative is to harmonise the figures so that they are identical for each co-producing country, to achieve that long-awaited official acceptance and payment of balances. To be clear, every project requires a sophisticated dossier that depends on special skill, built up

---

[*] Pierre Augustin Caron de Beaumarchais (1732-99). Writer, dramaturge, musician. One of the architects of the first law in favour of author's rights and founder of The Society of Authors.

over time. Marianne is an exceptional juggler in this acrobatic exercise.

But rules do also exist. We read contracts, we know how they are drawn up, where there are variables, the key issues. A thorough reading of a contract with a co-producer remains the basis of trust, the absolute opposite of "we trust each other, leave it at that", which is a relationship bound to end in conflict. It's not complicated, it just needs rigour and for our part this skill can never be delegated. This careful reading offers the chance to discuss all the points in great detail, but, above all, in our experience, to establish transparency from the outset as an essential element. Everything must be on the table. This is the same for all partners and also for the filmmakers. We refuse to separate the artistic from the economic, it must remain a coherent whole. The budget estimate must be understood by the filmmaker, a question of trust, of explaining costs if necessary and of managing balances and thus real margins for manoeuvre.

Detailed, transparent knowledge of the estimates and the resulting contracts is the pillar on which future management rests. This leads, for example, to our absolute refusal to use an agent. This is a condition. We would rather not make a film if the director insists on an agent, if we have to give up the in-depth dialogue on the relations between creation and its economy. From the first day to the last it is a coherent whole, right to the end of production. This can be painful, when money runs out, and the director must be asked to "make the effort" which, by the way, is rather unfair. Agents are unavoidable for actors, but that's another story: the collaboration is of a completely different nature and relies on a completely different timetable.

Bow tie

This desire to understand and not to delegate has guided us through the thirty-three years of our existence, so we have never needed a lawyer or any other legal expert, with one exception. Regrettably, this is not the case for our co-producer friends who delegate the legal side of things entirely. On one occasion there was a producer who was friendly and approachable but could not move without consultation. He would say "I've heard you, but I have to call my lawyer," "I've understood, I'm sorry, but I have to contact my production manager," etc., not to save time but simply because he did not know or control the decisive elements of the working process. He was totally dependent. No discussion was possible. We had to ask him to organise the meetings with his staff. Important to recall the fact that we deal with micro-businesses, with budgets of around a million and a half at best, often less, with the exception of two films which cost more than four million. However, in all cases the stakes are sufficiently limited that we don't need to call on outside expertise. No lawyer on our team and never the smallest claim, the slightest clash in any court, in over a hundred films.

The exception was a film in South Africa where a bank was involved for a decisive sum and the bank imposed on us both the creation of a specific company for the film and the intervention of a lawyer to do this. We chose him, we were under Anglo-Saxon jurisdiction. He was young and sympathetic but, from our point of view, imposed and unnecessary. At the end of the process, he simply earned about one and a half times more what we earned, the film's producers.

I remember this young and very nice English producer. We were co-producing a documentary. The contractual side was childishly simple. The film had to be made for around three hundred thousand euros, a comfortable budget. There was total trust between us. I had met him at a seminar I was running so there was no reason to complicate our lives. We were waiting for him to come to Paris to finalise the contractual relationship. And he was desperately postponing his trip. Finally, faced with these delays, we decide to go to London to see him. Eurostar, Waterloo and there he is, waiting for us, coming from the north of England with his hemmed shorts with large pockets and his trainers. He looks as if he is about to go on holiday. "Come on, we have an important meeting" he says. We land up at the foot of a large glass and metal tower, all sorts of solid gold plaques decorating the lobby, and we ascend to the 14th floor, to his lawyer's office. We meet a buttoned up, formal man, elegant with his bow tie, and here we are to discuss in polite and complacent turns of phrase this little contract of which all the details turn out to be very simple. An hour for nothing, and our friend Alex proudly tells us "I cut it short because the meter is running." We gently explain the uselessness of this meeting and that it would be more astute to read the contracts, understand them and ask the relevant questions so that he can still afford to take the Eurostar to Paris. The London atmosphere is lively, we are hungry and at this very moment Alex takes out of his backpack a small package, carefully wrapped. It is a sandwich "prepared by my wife", he announces. "In London everything is so expensive." What this signifies is that his tiny amount of money is financing a three-piece suit and a bow tie.

With very few exceptions, co-producers who have put us in the hands of lawyers have turned the working relationship into trench warfare and this, I

should add, almost always against the creative interests of the project and the quality of the relationship.
And even in these often-painful moments we don't
hire a lawyer. We settle these issues ourselves.

And to go a little deeper, the law and the contracts
are rarely in sync with the process of creation. We
should have sued this Portuguese producer who took
the liberty of asking us for twice as much as was clearly
written into the contracts. But the film was selected
for Cannes and to enter proceedings would have taken
one or two years and killed the film, so we gave in. Of
course, solid contracts are essential, but what remains
decisive is the care we take in choosing our partners.

I tease a young lawyer taking part for the second
time in one of our training sessions. "Last year, you
literally terrorised them, to the point that not one of
these producers could imagine taking a step without
a lawyer after your virtuoso intervention! We don't
invite you here to grow your own business. Quite the
opposite. We want your clear and precise presentation
to encourage them to read, learn and understand, so
that they will not need a lawyer, except of course in
emergencies."

Transparency remains a fantastic rule, though
not always simple to observe. Many colleagues are
opposed to it and practice being opaque which most
often serves as a basis for unequal and unfair treatment
at the heart of the whole tribe gathered to make a film.
As in all families, lack of transparency is very difficult
to sustain: everything is known, everyone talks to each
other on a film set- the co-producers, the partners
between themselves—so lack of transparency is thus
an ineffective exercise and often dangerous.

Incidentally, our detractors are wary of us because
we practice this transparency, systematically, in the

project of skills transferal. It is our absolute responsibility to relay and disseminate. Eight years as president of the Varan workshops, twenty years on the board of the Fémis, we were also involved from the start of the European programmes, in the creation of Eave*—with the magnificent Eckart Stein—and then of Eurodoc.† For Marianne as for me, that represents twenty years devoted to transferring skills to younger producers and directors.

The best dizi‡ in Tehran

But let's return to Iran. For almost three weeks we live with this absurd fear of not having a bank to produce this film. The refusals follow one after another, and once again we come up against collateral damage: rejections due not to Iran but simply because the business is considered too small. It's a sign of those times when most of the big banks take every opportunity to get rid of small clients. Finally, our very first historic banker gives us an opening for this Iranian film on the express condition that we do not carry out any transactions with Iran! Absurd as this is, we say nothing. The relief is immense, just to have an account, especially as this is one of the banks which specialises in cinema. A few small asides make it clear that it will probably only be temporary because an American investor is interested in the organisation, a rumour confirmed when we hear from the account manager

---

* European programme for development of fiction and documentary projects and TV series.

† Creative Europe programme offering workshops for development of documentary producers and their projects

‡ Dizy is a popular Iranian dish, a lamb and beef stew served in an earthenware pot

two weeks later, "If you had come today we wouldn't have been able to take you on."

We persevere in our marathon and the trail of small private banks working with Iran becomes clear. One of the two possible banks welcomes us. We open a second account. The space grows, the sky clears a little. The discussions now begin to clarify. The ideal would be to transfer funds before August 5th, the deadline for the second Trumpian cut-off after the one in May. This will be followed by a third one on November 4th, our banker informs us and he confirms that after this date nothing will be possible. This is impossible for us, the money is not in place, and the filming is scheduled to finish in the third week of October. We take a deep breath.

We have a completed script, financing in place, a solid team for the European part, a bank, two even, but still no partner in Iran, the second essential factor for the film to exist. The glimmer of a solution appears possible at the Berlin festival, so we prepare for a second trip. After the bitter failure of the first trip, Massoud panicked and turned to the first Iranian producer. He still holds the authorisation and having witnessed the disastrous F, offered his services again. Everything makes us believe that he is probably not the right man for the job: his position in the Farabi Cinema Foundation, his withdrawal from the production environment, his cheerful advice (F was his suggestion). We are becoming cautious, suspicious, very suspicious.

Our first film in Iran proved to be a disappointing experience particularly in the artistic domain. The producer at the time came from the establishment without any serious experience of production, of the terrain. He was upright, friendly and did not speak

a word of English. He came to Cannes to negotiate
our collaboration with his son, who translated. Then,
with three weeks to go before the shoot, we headed
to Tehran to finalise the most important creative
points, casting and technical crew. From our arrival
we noticed an energy unusual just a few weeks before
the start of shooting. At the first lunch, in one of
the famous dizi places of Tehran, in a lively, popular
atmosphere, Massoud and our dear producer, translated as usual through his son, announced that the
shoot would start on Saturday, two days late! We
were incredulous, we had good reason to be. Everything was locked in, we were going to pay dearly for
it—casting errors, a weak director of photography,
tension in the team—so many problems, especially
for a first film, problems that would continue to dog
the film until the end. "How can you do this to us?"
"The confusion comes from the calendar. We used the
Persian calendar, and you used the European one. It's
stupid, sorry." Unheard of for us, extravagant, surreal,
who would believe it, believe such an answer? We
who come from our little country, on our little plane,
at a date well-coordinated for the making of this film.
Very Iranian.

Therein lies another critical factor relevant to a
first work more than the second or third film and it
remains a considerable responsibility. Giving in on
decisive points has only limited consequences for us,
producers, but for the filmmaker it is his life that is at
stake. So not giving our all, doing everything we can, is
irresponsible. We aim to take a film to the top, to end
up in Cannes, Venice or Berlin. This means with near
certainty that the film will live on and that another one
might come into being. In each experience the stakes
are high.

We don't like the shooting stage: it's not the producers' time, it's the filmmaker's time. We usually say that if we have not made a mistake about the project, it's director, the crew, we have nothing to do on set. The only thing is just to make sure, a few days before the first days of shooting, that the power is in the hands of the director, which is not always the case. How many directors, when the time comes to act, panic and let the crew, a production manager or a DoP take over. We check that the main artistic decisions are the right ones and then we leave, not to stay and get caught up in the cables and inevitably cramp the filmmaker's freedom of movement. However, and this is fundamental, we demand that the rushes are synchronised straight away. To see the results on the screen from a distance (we have a large screen in the basement of our office) far from the atmosphere of the shoot, which is so exceptional, and from here to watch and communicate constantly, so prolonging the discussion started two, three or four years before this moment of 'action'. Then to return in a hurry, urgently, if there is a major problem, a conflict, and, finally, if the budget allows, to try and be present at the end. Physical presence is becoming increasingly rare given the tightness of funding.

Memories of Rithy Panh's first feature film in Cambodia.

A good script deeply rooted in reality, inspired by the characters of his documentary, just finished after almost two years maturing. At the time of the shoot, Rithy is literally tetanised. His return weighs heavily on him after his painful Pol Pot nightmare, a mission to revive Cambodian cinema on his shoulders, the anguish of action after a long preparation, the fear in his stomach imagining a helicopter will appear at any moment to swallow him up. How can I possibly understand? So many reasons. No particular production problems but he's busy with other things: buying the cobras, endless discussions about security, the night guard who drinks too much and eats the cobras (pretending they have escaped). Everything but diving in and concentrating on making his film. Evasion, immense difficulty in taking action, and naturally the small benevolent circle of the close team around him take charge. We are shooting on Super 16. The difficulty lies in how to view the rushes quickly. Given the travel time and the technical work it can easily take two weeks. So it takes us four weeks to get the measure of the disaster unfolding. The film was not being made, and for us, whatever the situation, it was better to have a shaky film from the filmmaker, whose critical project we had been working on together for more than two years, than a film "saved" by a production manager. Plane in a hurry. A night of discussions, cuts in the script, extension of the shooting time, release of the production manager, artistic fine-tuning with the team. It borders on physical confrontation. A very hard trip. Rithy shaves his head (a ritual) and changes elements of the cast, and the film finally lands on La Croisette in Competition.

We have been lucky enough over the last twenty years to share these often difficult journeys together. This changes everything. In Palestine, South Africa, Patagonia—how would we have succeeded if there hadn't been two of us?

Putting together the team is one of the key moments of this profession. This is a particularly acute issue for young filmmakers who do not have a team. The search is rooted in long collaboration and the situation of trust that results. The filmmaker has had enough time to understand that we are working in the interests of the film and exclusively for the film. He or she knows that the obligations and predators linked to finance will never take precedence over artistic values. Nourished by this long immersion, we look for the best solutions with an absolute rule, especially when a technician is very experienced, that there should be no power conflict, no power grab. Remember the production manager in Cambodia, the editor who, faced by a filmmaker making his first film, decided to become a school teacher? Foolish and unacceptable

There are, unfortunately, many such examples. The best people gather around a filmmaker and give everything they know to both filmmaker and the film. Not always easy, especially when you have to send a crew ten thousand kilometres away, for a 6-to-9-week shoot. We have had more good experiences than failures in this respect, and on several occasions we have come across skilled technicians who have given everything with rare generosity. The support at this precise time comes from friends (without work), family, the cousin or brother-in-law, the workman from home. You must think of nothing but the film. This leads us to unmistakeable forms of conservatism in our choices, and we favour repetition by returning to work with people we know. But we are also obliged to invent, to renew, to take risks, and the choice of collaborators demands that we watch the films, all the films where they have had a role, and to confer with those who have worked with these technicians, to compare experiences—in short, to leave nothing to chance. And if it is the filmmaker who decides, we know well that a decision of such importance cannot be taken during a two-hour meeting in a café. There is an element of chemistry at this key stage, of intuition, and yet you

have to put together what is best for the film. What is
true for the crew is also true for the cast.

Massoud wants Leila

Massoud wants Leila H for one of the main roles. He
wants Leila at all costs. We understand: she is a great
actress, undoubtedly one of the most talented in Iran
today, and at the same time we are holding back. We
find her a little old for the role and fear an ageing of the
ensemble. We discuss it, try to restrain his enthusiasm,
but without success, so we decide to get in touch
with this actress directly, as she does not want to go
through an agent. The opportunity arises and we go
to Berlin, where she is accompanying a film in competition. The appointment is made. In this luxury Berlin
hotel we meet a young woman, beautiful and gentle, a
far cry from the woman we have seen in her last films,
where she is tougher, more severe, more mature. We
fall under her spell. The discussion is simple, direct,
concrete and positive. Her husband, one of Iran's most
famous actors, a director and also a producer, happens
to be passing through. She introduces him and adds
mischievously, "You know A is a great producer." We
take note. The way forward is still in the balance, especially since Massoud has insisted on Leila to the very
end. And, frankly, this meeting makes us change our
minds.

The second trip is associated with the big international festival in Teheran, the Farj Film Festival. Our
prospective producer, responsible for international
relations at the Farabi Cinema Foundation, gives us
an official invitation. Red carpet, though everything
(plane, hotel) at our expense. This time, finally, the
reception at the airport should work better.

After each landing, as we leave the plane, we are diverted towards a greenish corridor with flickering neon lights where we are attended by portly men in odd shirts and braces. It is impossible to look them in the eye. These people are in charge of issuing our visa. First, we buy the insurance, deposit a form with our passports, and then begins an interminable wait. The men who took our passports disappear. Others emerge. There is an unmistakable feeling of random-ness. The previous trip, it was F's letter of invite which, not being endorsed by the ministry, kept us in this particularly uninviting place for two and a half hours. On the strength of our beautiful letter of invite we had cherished the sweet hope of getting out a little faster. We never understood why, but we were always the last to leave. Of course, we had made the banned film, the first one, so perhaps we are identified and marked by this venture? We decided to stay zen and on this occasion we got out after two hours. Progress. On the next trip we try the tourist strategy because from experience they are the ones who get out first. But they remind us that we are not tourists because on our last trip we had a festival invitation. "You aren't tourists. You must have a letter of invitation." We insist that this time we are just visiting friends with no professional purpose. The wait. Eventually we get out after an hour.

Our approach to Iran and its professional land-scape has gone through a rather radical transformation. Massoud, with his absolute art of avoidance, ambi-guity and invention, never stops explaining to us that nothing is possible in this country. The offer, in rela-tion to the producer we are going to see, is "the only one possible" given the context of Massoud's personal situation after the first film. Leila's husband does not have a good reputation. He is said to be expensive. All our searches for other leads, as described above, do not fit the regulations, and this country is in the hands of clans that block everything not to mention its rigorous system of political surveillance. On top of everything else, we are confronting another dead end since we can't produce this film without European technicians and actors due to stipulations in the recipe of rules imposed by the European contracts. And Massoud keeps telling us that for political, practical, security and professional reasons it is practically impossible to bring foreign technicians to Iran.

It takes the arrival of an Iranian sound engineer, resident in France, to sweep away this web of prohibitions that has been suffocating us for months. Dana[*] shoots from time to time in Iran. He tells us that there is absolutely no problem bringing in foreign technicians. Work visas are common and the chemistry of relations with Iranian professionals, always a delicate issue, works rather well. Dana opens up the network of Iranians in Europe (double passport) that we had started to explore earlier and so we find Babak,[†] an Iranian-Italian, for one of the key parts. We discover that our beautiful actress has a French passport and, above all, Dana puts us in contact with the core of an embryonic team that suddenly feels normal, professional, and all register as casual workers.

And so to A, Leila's husband, whom we met in Berlin. We unravel the fabric of Massoud's inventions on almost every point that has plagued us these past months: "the internet doesn't work here, or it's really bad; be careful, no information in the newspapers;

---

[*] Dana Farzanehpour.
[†] Babak Karimi, a former editor who has become one of the most important actors in Iran today.

we're not going to be able to get the information we need; I'm not sure you can come after producing the first film, it's risky." Not to mention his incessant pressure to get the filming brought forward: "The authorisation expires in December, after that it's dead; after the elections it will be impossible; Leila is only free in April, after that she has another film", and so on, again and again. But it's the boy who cried wolf. We love him but we haven't believed him for a long time. A perilous game, because you never know, perhaps one time...

Of course, this is only his second film, he hasn't "piloted the Boeing" for seven years. The wait has been endless and his anxiety on so many issues is at its peak. During the trip at the end of July, seized by panic, he makes some totally delusional proposals for the core cast. We unpick them, listen, try to sort things out. Above all we undertake to follow up each choice. We resume discussions on the essentials at each stage, checking changes in the script in the final stretch, what needs adjustment once the actors are signed — in short, protecting Massoud, protecting the film, against this mass of pressure. He knows at the end of July — first shoot in mid-August — that if the lead actress is not found we are ready to delay the whole thing, which would have been catastrophic, if only for reasons linked to an increasingly severe embargo. The key focus is the film. Without certainty everything can collapse and we have to work out how, in extremis, to find a solution.

But let's return to the meeting with this producer during the Fajr festival, a key trip, because without an Iranian partner in these early spring days, there is no film. This time we land in another galaxy. T gives us an appointment in the midst of this great assembly of Iranian cinema, the one and only international festival, a little thin on foreign participation due to the embargo but all the symptoms of a great festival are here. Everything is held in an ultramodern mall. On the ground floor luxury shops. On the first floor more than a thousand square metres of mobile phone shops, the big brands all present. On the second floor an identical area entirely dedicated to the protective cases for the phones bought on the floor below. On the third, a myriad of restaurants and finally on the fourth, equipped with a pass, we access the festival reception. The meeting point is set in a bar, a bit out of the way. Everything is done to inflate the head man: rumour has it that he's powerful, that nothing can be done without his blessing. A charged atmosphere for this first meeting and T doesn't arrive. We are told that his commitments are difficult, a little extra pressure. We almost feel guilty. After more than an hour's delay he finally appears, in a wheelchair manoeuvred by a very tall man with dark glasses, and the heavily handicapped man instantly reveals himself to be the classic apparatchik—personable, correct, measured, skilful. The interview remains formal, friendly but totally inconsistent. First contact.

An appointment is made for the next day to talk about serious matters. This time T receives us in his office in the northern district, where the Tehranese upper-middle class lives, a huge district of metal and glass surrounded by flamboyant neo-classical stone buildings. Rolls, Maseratis, all the luxury of the planet is here. His office sends a driver. This is not our world, our lifestyle, our cinema… but so be it. We remain on guard. He receives us with his partner, the man in charge of production. T speaks English, his colleague not a word. Massoud is there, our eyes meet. He's uncomfortable, he senses our unease. This time the discussion is more direct, not a word about the failure of F. T wants to make the film but for reasons that are obvious it is this right-hand man, this colleague, who is in charge. Then everything changes—horror. This man is unable to look Marianne, a woman, in the eye. When she asks questions it is to T that he answers. We tackle the question, key for us, of the Iranian costs. "No problem, I can give you a quote right now, right here in this office." "But you haven't read the screenplay?" "You don't need to read the screenplay to give a quote." The temperature goes up a notch. We talk about our constraints, our European obligations for the crew. "But then why are you making the film in Iran? Why aren't you shooting in Europe?" It's dead. Unimaginable to make a film with these people. He's right, better to shoot in Greece than work with this individual.

We remain polite until the end. Once again we are offered dry cakes and art books, the protocol has to be respected, but it's over. Fortunately, thanks to Dana, our French-Iranian sound engineer, a plan B takes shape, one that revolves around A, Leila's husband, whom we met in Berlin. We leave T with the promise to meet again "as soon as possible" to make decisions...

We must change hotel. Ours is closing for renovation. Well, it was already half closed. Huge empty halls, with men, always silent, slumped in skai sofas, deep and warped, watching religious programmes all day long. The swimming pool empty for years, overrun by vegetation. A dodgy lift, but like most of them, awash with plaintive and metallic religious music. We could start writing a small guide to Tehran's hotel industry: its garlic and jujuba shampoos; its mobile phone recharging stations bearing the effigy of the Supreme Leader, aptly named Supercharger; its systematic absence of bedside lamps (we aren't supposed to read at night in these places); the undeniable success of brown, the colour of goose shit and olive green; its desperately empty minibars; the bitter struggle to get a second sachet of instant coffee every morning and its inevitable basement breakfast rooms always lit by flickering neon. During the shoot we move upmarket. At first, we are literally surrounded, in a complex located at the crossroads of four urban highways, "so you can get to the set quickly" explains the manager. Then finally we land up in a real rococo Persian palace, all in flaming carmine haunted by the great Darius.

We migrate, taking up the opportunity to be closer to A's offices. And at our first breakfast, in the basement, we land in a room occupied by about thirty young women, strictly veiled in black, all accompanied by a father or husband, their faces covered with the same white bandage. It is striking. Where are we? We discover that the hotel is located opposite the main plastic surgery clinic in the capital. It turns out that the overwhelming majority of young Iranian women trade their beautiful curved noses for trumpet-shaped ones, American-style; a real massacre, the influence of cinema. Throughout our days, we cannot avoid pointing out, mischievously, the rare authentic appendages that have somehow escaped the scalpel.

We meet K, Dana's friend, and everything becomes clearer. We finally meet normal people who talk about cinema. K leads us to A. The discussion turns out to be simple, almost too simple. We can't believe it, it's like a small miracle. We sign the next day, but we have to get rid of T and to do it diplomatically. This man has the power, and the right, to give life or death to the film. Permission to shoot lies in his hands. A new meeting is set up to settle everything. And here I draw on my past as an activist to find the right words, extreme politeness, cordiality, flattery. Nobody is fooled, but we tell him that it will no longer be him making the film but this young producer, whom he knows well. He grasps the situation immediately and, well, finds it an excellent idea. He is too powerful to be fooled or to show what he really thinks.

There were still many twists and turns ahead, and a definite resistance to conceding the film authorisation, but finally, at the end of July, we obtain a new permit. It may seem insignificant but without it the film is dead, regardless of whether everything is in place, ready to go—crew, cast, six co-producers, commitments on all sides, contracts signed, financing on the way to being settled, a good two hundred thousand euros already committed. Perhaps we are a bit crazy.

You need strong nerves. We are making prototypes. No two films are alike though the experiences overlap. That long awaited call from a tv channel, for three hundred or six hundred thousand euros. Just hearing the ring you know that the answer is at hand, so close. "We can't back you after all, sorry." This kind of experience, and so many others. We treat ourselves to two days of Iranian holiday, finally leaving Tehran and heading for Kashan and Isfahan. It is a sublime trip in two cities of extreme beauty, in a country without tourists. We discover the kindness of these people who we were beginning to dislike.

Acrobatic dives

The bank that closed our account has struck again. We have been waiting for a transfer from Italy for a long time. The mere name of Yalda on the order results in rejection of the transfer. It's the twenty-eighth of June and we're shooting in two months' time. These thirty thousand euros are vital and they have disappeared, swallowed up in the mysteries of an impenetrable banking system. They eventually resurface at the end of August but four days before the shoot they are still not in our account.

Yes, we leave tomorrow. We shoot in four days' time. Through a series of risky double somersaults we succeed in transferring what we have already committed to paying—small amounts of cash here and there, covering for our own comings and goings, the crew's travel. We're helped by Swiss friends, transfers into the Czech account of our dear producer and finally a French bank that functions effectively. It's one of those small private banks that specialise, among other things, in working with countries under embargo, protected by the French authorities. Invaluable.

Among all the joyful news, the most astonishing news is the departure, two weeks before the shoot, of dear Leila, the support role. She has been Massoud's dream for two years, wife of our Iranian partner, absolute star in her country, contract signed and first deadline paid. It's complete madness, unheard of, even for us. The email she sends rings false. She mentions doubts about the part. Obviously, it's not the principle role. We'll probably learn the real reason for her decision soon enough but for now it's just a bombshell during preparations which appeared to be advancing well. We bounce back. Bhenaz Jafari, a formidable actress whom we had just seen in Cannes in Panahi's beautiful film[*] and who had appeared in Massoud's first feature film, has agreed to play a small role in *Yalda*. She liked the project and it was immediately obvious to Massoud (and to us) that she was perfect for the role of Mona which Leila had just deserted.

Apart from this, the most striking episode is a classic—unexpected but classic. The day before, the team have to pick up all the electrical equipment to carry out the 'prelights', or, as we say in French 'installer la lumière' for the shoot. Everything has been sourced from one supplier, so we are vulnerable. And we discover that K has obtained a quote, but never completed the deal. The company, faced with a foreign—read wealthy—film, increases its price nine-fold at the point of collection. Subtle. This represents a quarter of the budget for our shoot in Iran which is already four or five times the price it would be in France or Germany. We have faced this kind of manoeuvre before but never on such a scale. Confronted by this kind of attitude, for ethical and economic reasons and out of respect for the whole crew, we do not give in. We have sometimes chosen to lose a lot of money (in our terms, of course) rather than give in to such black-mail by companies, co-producers and filmmakers. In this case the risk is significant: postponement of the start of shooting with all the consequences—crew, set, various commitments—but we have to face it down. Two days of crisis, two days to put in place alternative solutions: bringing in equipment from Turkey, doing the rounds of the equipment rental companies again, including those in the provinces, reducing the list of equipment. Everyone works on it. The end seems to be in sight. We are leaving the next day.

---

[*] *Three Faces*, 2018, directed by Jafar Panahi.

The shoot

For *Yalda* we took far more risks than usual, if only in the choice of the core elements, those that make the film beyond the filmmaker and a great screenplay. In short, the actresses, the actors, the cinematographer and the editor. Of course, the others are all important but this small group is decisive. Get the lead role wrong and the film collapses; get the support roles wrong and the edit becomes an impossible acrobatic feat because you have to cut out anything that falls short without hesitation, risking the overall coherence and sense of the film; get the cinematographer wrong and the whole thing plunges into a version of desperation. For *Yalda*, as previously mentioned, we are still missing the actress for the principal role at the end of July, with the shoot now planned for the beginning of September.

We've had earlier experiences of this sort, to the point where we have become "authoritarian" producers; authoritarian in the sense of protecting an edifice, that has taken three, four, five years to build, from collapsing in the final weeks. This is the time for 'close' protection of the filmmaker—not to give in without certainty that we can live with the main actor for ninety or a hundred minutes, otherwise there's no film. Authoritarian, too, because of our experience, accumulated over forty-two feature films. These experiences give rise to gut certainties. The decision to change the lead role in *Lumumba* in the last few weeks, taken by the director but under pressure of recurrent doubts over the initial choice. The choice of actress for Pablo Aguero's first film, for the role of his mother. For months he carries out screen tests with non-professionals in the hope of finding this mother, tests that prove hopeless. The impasse is obvious, so we keep suggesting that he choose from among the great Argentinian actresses with the rationale that for a first film, and such a delicate role, it would be better to have a Stradivarius than dream of some beautiful and unlikely young woman from Patagonia who will have to learn from scratch. After six months, bingo. Pablo falls in love with one of the most interesting actresses in the country. We would have preferred someone else but what followed proves him right and he finally ends up with a remarkable first film on La Croisette.*

We had just experienced a similar story with the film of the magnificent Chilean director, Fernando Guzzoni. Everything depended on finding a young boy of eighteen. Intelligence and the defence of his own interests make the filmmaker intransigent. Two hundred, four hundred, six hundred boys and nothing is decided. But change is always possible as the shoot gets closer. We are completely involved. Fernando knows that we are only defending his interests. He consults us knowing himself that he hasn't found a solution. And in the last few weeks the boy appears, magical, as clear to the filmmaker as it is to us, a magnificent actor and, by the end, a great film.†

With the last film, *Sow the Wind*, released after *Yalda*, we have to go to breaking point. This is the first time in our experience and that's no accident because in film after film the same situations keep occurring. Danilo is looking for a 22-year-old woman for the lead role and she will be on screen from the first to the last frame. She is an atypical character, mute, deep, all interiority. If he doesn't find her, we can assume

* *Salamandra* with Dolores Fonzi—Directors' Fortnight 2008.
† *Jesus*, with Nicolas Duran—Competition at the San Sebastian Film Festival—Jba Production 2016.

there is no film. He looks at hundreds of women, for more than a year, and if some seem promising none are convincing and the overwhelming majority reflect a very contemporary archetype; young girls, already shaped, having lost a certain truth, a naturalness necessary for the role. In desperation we suggest that Danilo tries the girl from Alice Rohrwacher's first film.[*] She was twelve years old at the time with this natural authenticity intact. He doesn't object to the idea. He looks for her. She lives in the Tuscan countryside in the 'Elf community.' He finds her and films her. These tests surprise everyone. Yile has the ability to touch a radiator and to make us believe that it's a tree. She inspires trust and an uncommon sensitivity. We believe in her: Marianne and I are totally convinced that she's the one. But Danilo, although not unappreciative of her, insists on a girl with an Apulian accent and Yile speaks with a Tuscan accent. He is right. This is a wholly legitimate aim, a matter of credibility for the Italian audience.

With one month to go before the shoot, we find ourselves back at square one. Danilo is still desperately searching. And the pressure, the anguish, the necessity all lead, inevitably, to the encounter he is searching for. We watch the tests and, once again, are faced with the terrible responsibility of protecting a filmmaker, the film, five years of work. His preference is impossible. So we have to overstep our role and set in motion an undesirable blackmail to impose Yile. It's incredibly risky. In response to this domineering approach he might take against the young actress. We could be seriously mistaken and she might turn out to be incapable of playing this role, she's not a professional. Moreover,

---

[*] *Corpo Celeste* with Yile Vianello—Directors' Fortnight Cannes 2011—Tempesta/JBA Production..

he fears her—she's too free, with an uncontrollable wildness and spirit. We are in Paris, he is in Puglia, and it's the eve of the shoot. The trust between us remains absolute. He knows that we are fiercely defending his film. And with our faith in the trust forged during the past four years, in the certainty that everything might collapse if we accept his latest proposal, we say to him, "It's Yile or we abandon ship. You can make the film with Italy alone, but not with us."

Plane to Bari. Danilo is clever. He knows as well as we do that this young girl is the best solution, so he takes the plunge imposing a condition—to be able to dub her voice. He has the wisdom to shoot the first week of exteriors with her alone, with a reduced crew, to get closer to her, to tame her. And the miracle happens. They are in the same film, in the same story. Yile, luminous, understands everything. In the end, to dub has no meaning. The role is silent: a deep voice, unique and her look does the rest. For Danilo, who has been working on this story for more than five years, *Sow the Wind* is 'the' film, a very beautiful film that lands in the official selection at Berlin.

With Massoud, his anxiety is at its peak. Everything is in place. The shooting is to start in four weeks' time and still there's no solution for the main role. He even comes up with crazy proposals which he turns into theories, "She must have had a child to understand the role." We're not getting very far. Numerous casting sessions without success. Far from the site of action, we immerse ourselves in Iranian films, whatever is accessible. This is a very effective method because in a film, whatever the role, the actress reveals herself, far more than in a screen test held in an office. And we spot her. "I know her and I've discounted her. She's too young," he tells us. "Watch her again.

To us she seems an obvious choice." Massoud meets her, spends two hours with her, and comes out overwhelmed by the strength of this young actress and her ability to grasp the role. He beams and says, "She even suggested some incredibly accurate dialogue without even having read the script." Immense relief. Sadaf will play in this film alongside an exceptional Behnaz Jafari who, at short notice, takes the place of Leila, the bird who took flight at the last moment. Miracle and magic of cinema.

The shoot. This time all our theories collapse, a house of cards. It's clear that we have to be there. The set-up is definitely atypical: the whole shoot in one location, two actresses carrying the film, a German-Bulgarian cinematographer brought in by the vagaries of production agreements. We have seen all his work but Iran is a long way away. How is this strong personality going to give his all to the film-maker and at the same time find the resources to work together with the Iranian camera crew?

We are in a single location: a vast theatre complex with one large stage, and around it seven smaller stages — offices, technical facilities, everything we need. The place is a mirage, the illusion of a government plan to create a vast theatre hub in the popular part of the city, south of Tehran, a cultural centre for the people. But it proves a total failure, brand new and empty. The whole film can be shot in these deserted spaces. We also set up the edit room here because we have been experimenting with editing alongside the shoot on several films with great success. Shoots are becoming shorter and shorter, a question of finance. Working in a single location, with actors available without real time limits, allows for all the adjustments (the reshoots, the work on rhythm) which result from each morning's screening and critique of the rushes, director, principal editor, cinematographer and producers all viewing together.

If at certain moments of this epic journey we had concerns, doubts about the ability of this filmmaker to take this screenplay much further, this shoot sweeps everything away. Massoud proves to be strong, attentive, focused on the essential: a great filmmaker. It's a kind of welcome bonus to recognise, finally, that he is indeed the director we hoped for.

Ultimately, the experience of collaboration between the European and Iranian crew goes well: everyone finds their own way. Julian[*] immerses himself, absorbs and translates Massoud's wishes with skill and intelligence, and the relation with the editor[†] is fluid, joyful, rare. But the most unusual experience is undoubtedly that of Helder, our Portuguese-Luxembourgish chief electrician, a small miracle delivered by the co-production deal with Luxembourg. We feared the worst but finally landed up with an exceptional young man. The Iranians will not forget him any time soon.

Iranian electricians store cables, fittings, plugs, filters—everything—in big deep boxes. Every time Helder asks for something they empty everything out to find it. These boxes are also very heavy, so it takes three people to move them. With an astute plan, our friend organises a storage system where small boxes are suspended in the big one and, above all, he gets them to find the wheels. Liberation. The relief can be read in the eyes of his team. It's simple. They didn't

---

[*] Julian Atanassov, DoP and cameraman of *Yalda*.

[†] Jacques Comets, principal editor of *Yalda*. This is the second time we have edited alongside him—after Palestine—and the eighth film we have made together.

really need Helder to do this but they haven't done it before because this is how they've been making films for years. And Helder saves lives. Not a single suspended spotlight comes with a safety device. He requires that these are fitted. Most of the connections are made with exposed, deadly wires. He insists that plugs are used and above all has connection boxes made. To save money the technicians do not have any spare bulbs on the set. A lamp breaks and it's two to three hours, depending on the infernal traffic of this city, before the crew can start again. Helder orders replacement bulbs. And the cherry on the cake— Helder is a vegan. The canteen pays so much attention to this that his entire team ends up eating vegan. The story is without end, a tale of encounter and learning between working cultures.

The Iranians work seven days a week on a film set. Their notion of time has little to do with ours, not to mention the problems of punctuality due to traffic jams. Dana, the Iranian sound engineer, who lives and works in France, gets stuck in traffic jams and dutifully calls the production team to inform them that he will be ten minutes late. "Don't worry, you'll still be the first to arrive," jokes the first assistant. It's a large film industry (more than a hundred films are shot in Iran every year) and it works. It's just not under the same pressure of efficiency, of time management, especially because by far the majority of the crew, to our great surprise, is appallingly badly paid. The hierarchy of salaries is staggering, benefiting the few heads of section, the production and especially the actors. The rules of the market on the one hand and a poorly protected profession on the other. I remember our scandalised reaction when we learned in Cambodia that the extras were paid $1 a day. We protested and the response came back: "A high school teacher earns $16 a month. What this regime grants to our extras is already a privilege." Sensitive cultural issues which, in such cases, don't favour transparency.

Shoots always go well — well, almost

Back to Palestine. Last-but-one week of the shoot for *Salt of this Sea*. The team is exhausted and tense. We are shooting in Israel and it so happens that Annemarie, the director, has lost her passport. The key sequence of the film, the arrest, has just been filmed. Magic. The team collapses in tears of relief. The French production manager, the only person authorised to deal with customs, sends the rushes to the Schwartz laboratory (we should have been wary) in Switzerland. It's part of the co-production agreement. Tuesday night, black Tuesday. The S16mm rushes go into the baths on Thursday morning but then get left there when the machine breaks down. Drama.

We phone Annemarie, who collapses. The work schedule is reviewed. There is only one rest day before the shoot ends, the exact same day that the main actress, a Palestinian-American, is due to leave as her visa expires. The decision is made to reshoot this essential sequence in Haifa, whatever the cost. The application for authorisation is in progress but the clock is ticking and no response is forthcoming. On Saturday, the decision is made to shoot the sequence on Monday, with or without permission. The team is in place, the machine is back on the road. A particularly angry man, surrounded by a group of thugs, disrupts the shoot. Tension rises. The first assistant loses it and starts shouting in Arabic. A full-scale brawl breaks out. Everyone runs for cover — grabbing the camera, the equipment, the costumes—and in the chaos an extra gets his nose smashed. Annemarie has reached her limit. The lead actress goes on strike and refuses to film anything more. Negotiations are going on around the clock. Annemarie panics, thinks that the scene will never be reshot, starts talking about a deliberate plot. We reassure her but the heartache and exhaustion are immense. We promise to find a solution during post-production, that we will shoot this sequence along with all the other pickups needed for the film. It's settled. The story could have ended there but a registered letter from a lawyer demands 100,000 euros for the damaged nose of one extra!

The shooting of the arrest eventually takes place in Marseille during the edit. When we ask the audience about this sequence, shot in France, nobody has noticed the difference. Magic of cinema.

In all these years, we have never had an irreversible disaster which is very surprising. And yet, in the twenty or so countries we have been to, nothing has been simple. The Argentinians are over-unionised. The director of photography[*] complains that at 25 years old, they behave worse than the oldest hands of the SFP.[†] At 6 o'clock sharp there's a phone call from the union asking them to cut the power. It's all the more absurd as they are filming two thousand kilometres away from Buenos Aires, at the end of the world, in a village as sad as death where there are two forlorn cafés that close at dusk.

---

[*] The magnificent Hélène Louvart, with whom we had the pleasure to collaborate on six features.

[†] Societe Francaise de Production (the French Production Company), famous producer of public service television, often criticised for its heavy-handed attitude towards unions.

The South Africans are models of luxury. They work all year round for American or European films shot in South Africa and are therefore highly competent and very expensive. Exception is made for heads of departments (DoP, line producers, sound) where, according to the best post-colonial tradition, foreign producers stand firm and so they are imported. It is impossible for a young South African filmmaker to have his own team due to his precarious finances. And if by any chance a production team accepts a local and ultra-low paid film crew, it risks seeing it head off at any moment to make a commercial for the Americans. We had this bitter experience on Ramadan's film, the first feature made by a black director in this country.* This was in 1996 but it might as well have been yesterday. In the middle of the shoot half the crew disappeared to join the blockbuster, *Tarzan*.

In Papua New Guinea it was another story. Only Australian films are shot here, with crocodiles as stars, and we have to invent solutions with magnificent people who are only just discovering cinema and, for the record, we have to use guards armed with bows and arrows to protect the equipment. Séverin† accompanies one of these guards to his bank to withdraw some money before going back to his village. The man can neither read nor write. He's greeted by a small bespectacled boy behind the counter. He has a sharp haircut and European-style clothing. The young Papua New Guinean guard approaches the counter and whispers into the ear of this young bureaucrat who immediately hits the computer keys to carry out the transaction. On leaving, Séverin, incredulous, asks our guard what he whispered, and he replies, "Sweet

---

* *Fools*. Silver Leopard at the 1997 Locarno Festival.

† Séverin Blanchet see note page 18

potato… my password." Chasms between us and the daily life of this strange country some of whose villages only made first contact with "civilisation"* about a century ago.

In Palestine, there's a multitudinous team. Films are so rare here and they have a surprising characteristic: all the co-workers, from technicians to trainees, from stage management to set design, call themselves directors in their CVs.

Second birth—the edit

Then comes the edit, a stage of critical importance. It is the moment where we rediscover the intimacy which gets lost in the turbulence of the shoot. It's the chance to go back and explore all the fundamentals of the film. We love this moment of rediscovery.

It's the second birth of the film. All the questions, doubts, problems and delights that surfaced during the writing - the choice of crew, casting, the shoot - everything resurfaces with no room for complacency and at this stage, with no possibility of going back: it's too late. It's a stage where it's imperative to forget the screenplay, and to engage this skill, this need to reinvent the film according to what has now been shot, what's there, in the image. We have seen the rushes, we must view everything and try to make a realistic assessment of the film, to project it as far as it can go, without deluding ourselves.

And then, a precious moment, the filmmaker and his/her editor must be given time to immerse themselves, to grapple with the multiple problems that emerge, up to the first edit—that two-to-three-

---

* See First Contact, the magnificent first part of a trilogy by Bob Connolly and Robin Anderson (1982).

hour beast which reveals everything. It's a fragile and contradictory moment, volatile, full of hope and despair. This is the moment when we return. The discussion at this point proves essential, informed by a total candour. For too long now we've been skirting around all these questions. The editor is sometimes surprised by the lack of subtlety in our exchanges. The filmmaker often loses his or her critical judgement at first—not always—and the editor takes over.

Exceptionally, we have experienced the opposite phenomenon. A filmmaker who suddenly becomes brutal with his material. He takes a dislike to it and mishandles it. The editing goes much too fast: a whole section of the story literally eliminated, jeopardising the film. This phenomenon, which is rare, results from a shoot that has been too tough, a period when the filmmaker suffers a lot. The rushes bring everything back and he can't stand it. We are far away, following the edit from a distance, transferring files every three or four days, viewing and then communicating by Skype. We are forced to stop everything, to suggest a break, to pause the process and then to start again by going back to the original rushes. It will take a few weeks for the filmmaker to regain a sense of direction, to discover the potential of his material and finally to deliver the film in all its strength. There will still be a lot of back and forth but the film will follow the grain of its material, not work against it.

Then the editor takes over. The trust built up enables the film to move forward and, once the structure is in place, everything can be removed that is inessential or detracts from the film: weaknesses in the direction, the inadequacy of certain actors (often in the supporting roles cast at the last minute), over-attachment to certain scenes, an actor, a line, a situation, for reasons far removed from the work in progress. Where something is essential to the story there's the challenge of finding alternative solutions. We have even experienced a co-producer's intervention: "We can't cut this scene. It cost us a fortune." Then the editor's critical judgement runs out, exhausted by the filmmaker's resistance in the face of each loss. We are still quite fresh, schooled by years of collaboration, and we are still able to intervene in the final choices.

It's so difficult to know who is right in these final moments but here too experience plays a part. We have been through so many magnificent battles at the end of the edit, often real horse-trading. Debates that start with a cut at two hours and twenty minutes, the filmmaker insisting nothing more can be cut, and end up with a cut at one hour and forty minutes. There are shots we have fought for to the bitter end, winning ninety percent of them and giving in on one, and then the filmmaker—after the negative is cut, the film screened at Cannes, a 35 mm print—asks that we take out this same shot. There are as many stories as there are films, but we can attest that not a single edit has ended against the wishes of the filmmaker. We have always arrived at consent, complete satisfaction, and no trace of bitterness over any loss.

No film can be made against the material, against the filmmaker. I remember the head of Arte losing it over the interminable edit of a documentary, twelve months long, which followed a shoot that had lasted eighteen months with a profoundly hesitant, elusive, searching filmmaker. In July, unable to take it anymore, he proposed to 'Markerise'[*] the situation (a barbaric term), to finish it off once and for all—the material is magnificent—by adding an eloquent script.

[*] In reference to Chris Marker, genius of text, collage and editing

The English co-producers had already cracked two months earlier and finished the film with the skill which is their speciality. They take the edit in progress and recut it, forcing connections and links through commentary. A massacre and, needless to say, the film was broadcast on their channel in two parts of 52 minutes, at midnight! Arte, which stays closer to its films, held on for another two months. We didn't give up. At the end of September, the edit was finally complete with the director and editor still on board. The result is exceptional and wins the Fipa prize in January. Arte likes the film (the attempt to speed it up in July now long forgotten) and in March we receive a phone call from the English channel asking to buy the film. "But you co-produced it and you've already broadcast it!"* Good films are not made against their directors.

In Tehran, following the shoot, a first cut is in place. It's full of structural and rhythmic problems but the film is there, without a doubt. All the material is sent back to France without any difficulty, except for the absurd story of the back-up drives which disappear, left behind in a pistachio shop by a co-production partner visiting the shoot. There will be a few more weeks of fine-tuning in Paris. The collaboration between the editor and the filmmaker remains fluent. They have already worked together on the first film.

With this previous film it had started out very badly. Massoud, taking everyone by surprise, had arrived in Paris with the film "edited." A surprise gift. "Yes, I had some time and I got started with a friend who is an editor and we almost finished it." We were

---

* Channel 4 version broadcast in 1997, The Bank, the President and the Pearl of Africa. Arte's version, Our Friends at the Bank

taken aback to say the least, and worried, but we did watch it. At the end of this viewing we asked Comets,[*] the French editor, to get to work and above all not to look at what Massoud had kindly concocted for us, which was unusable. They then learned to work together and for the filmmaker, it was his first film, it was a wonderful discovery of what a great editor can bring to a film.

It is sometimes said that it is useful for an editor to speak the language of the film he is editing. This is undoubtedly an asset, but it is far more important to have a great editor who doesn't speak the language, than just a good one who does. They enter into the music, they grasp everything quickly, they can even cut the image made in this language that they don't speak. This same editor, Comets, worked with Tsai Ming-Liang, who only speaks Chinese, and it was a pleasure to see them struggle for hours over the cut of three images with complete understanding and without exchanging a word.

Landing

Then comes post-production, a series of stages, each of which is essential to the fine tuning of the work in progress. For *Yalda*, special effects. We are immersed in green screens[†] and it is essential to monitor them because the broadcast transmission is on-screen all the time so any slight change in the edit means everything else needs adjustment. Colour grading. A lot of questions about the balance

---

[*] Jacques Comets, editor of more than forty feature films and, for twenty years, head of the editing department at La Fémis film school in Paris.

[†] A technique that allows the images of the programme to be inserted on all the screens in the set.

between the set and the backstage area. It appears simple but in this case the shifts from one to the other happen constantly. And, finally, sound.

It's an essential stage in this second birth—establishing the film's sound universe. The sound edit allows for the enriching of the sync sound, for work on the off-screen sound, and to reinvent and reinterpret the score that the picture edit has just created. Sound effects allow us to complement and enhance what may be missing in the sync sound and above all to prepare the soundtracks that will be used for dubbing.

We have had some magical moments of creativity with sound, the last one between Danilo* and this great Dane, a brilliant creator with an inordinate talent, but with a disorganisation that sometimes brings us to the edge of a nervous breakdown. To see it through we have to repatriate both the bird and its thousands of tracks to Paris (often the case). A madness but we have to distance him from all other projects and his chaotic shared childcare arrangements. Away from everything, Danilo and Peter† discover each other but above all they play with sound like two children free to imagine the unimaginable, free to have fun and to achieve what Danilo would not have thought possible.

To this can be added the thousand-and-one adventures with the music. It's a stage that is always complicated because it is too often left to the last, whether in relation to original composition, the painful replacement of the provisional music used during the edit or because of rights negotiations, which usually prove tortuous and full of surprises. There was the brilliant performance of the Korean, Kpop, for the opening of

---

* Danilo Caputo, Italian filmmaker from Puglia, director of *Sow the Wind*, JBA Production, Berlin Panorama 2020.
† Peter Albretchsen Danish sound designer

Fernando Guzzoni's Chilean film.[*] "I graduated in law, I know about rights, there's no problem," our co-producer tells us. We insist, do a search on the main piece of music and discover that it has a modest twenty million views on YouTube: that's to say it's completely unusable. To save the film's opening music we have to negotiate hard in Seoul, with the opportune support of the French embassy, but we are forced to replace all the other tracks by Kpop at the beginning of the film with tracks from a music bank, a particularly painful operation for the director, coming at the end of the editing process. It's reminiscent of the nightmare negotiating Quilapayun's music, essential to Patricio Guzman's film, *Salvador Allende*. The group had broken up with lawsuits, one against the other, in the period just after the Popular Unity government. Another time there was the 33rpm record unearthed in a junk shop by the set designers of Marc Recha's film.[†] The film had been mixed, it had screened in Cannes, and then we discovered that the music publisher had been in litigation for years with the composer and that it was impossible to use this track from the depths of time. A remix, new optical transfer, new internegative, new copies...

Rights management is always simpler with original music but the experience, with rare exceptions, remains laborious and unsatisfactory, all too often long-drawn-out and too late. There are some fine exceptions, Marc Marder for example, the musician in all of Rithy Panh's films. His engagement is deep, the relationship goes way back, and the result is always strong and profound.

---

[*] *Jesus* by Fernando Guzzoni 2018.
[†] *Les Mains Vides* by Marc Recha 2003

Finally, there's the mix, another essential link in the completion of the film. Another time of reinterpretation with the mixer's hands playing with all that sound can offer. The presence of the editor at the mixing stage remains non-negotiable. This allows the editor the possibility of cutting, reversing or extending a shot, if necessary, right up to the last moment. This presence is often vital for the final decisions on the music mix, a critical moment in which we always participate.

It's so difficult to expect a deep commitment from someone who appears fleetingly for a sound edit or the final mix, whilst we've been involved for a couple for years. Here again, the quality of the people remains decisive. Co-production obliges us to work with countries where the sound culture can be different to ours. We were surprised to discover, for example, that in Spain or the Netherlands they mix in a fortnight, whereas in France we find it difficult to complete under three weeks. Another time we find a sound editor from a large neighbouring country whose eyes open wide when we raise with him the absence of 'non-sync' sound in his edit. "It's raining outside. We're in a church with a tin roof. Perhaps we should add some sounds of rain to lead into the next shot where we come out of the church?" Our experience, bound by co-production obligations, is not always a happy one. On the sound for *Yalda*, the relationship with our partners was delicate and, though it's hard to admit, each projection still leaves us now with an uncomfortable sense of dissatisfaction. Sometimes we go for a remix but the budgets are so tight that it often makes this impossible.

Finally, again due to the constraints of co-production, there is the nightmare of having to deliver in various media, often using several laboratories which are not up to scratch, far from the film, far too far away altogether, and where they are specialists at constantly passing the buck—so much simpler. This mania for never being wrong is strange. It's a very contemporary thing. We can't remember it being like this ten or twenty years ago. It's become a general sport, inventing things. The most outlandish excuses, twists and turns, just to escape saying "We were wrong." Perhaps it's the result of being monitored all the time, everywhere. Disconcerting and unacceptable.

Then comes the time for subtitling, a stage that requires ruthlessness regarding skills. You can't spend your time reading a film yet everything has to be there. Once again, it is crucial to work with the best. Never let a professional subtitle in a language that is not their mother tongue, not least because, let's be honest, in most cases we are not best qualified to judge a translation. Whether for subtitling or for a screenplay, a bad translation kills the text. For screenplays we have got into the habit of seeking out the translator of our favourite books in the language to be translated. For the Portuguese translation, we went looking for the French translator of Portuguese novelist António Lobo Antunes. The writing was superb. It was published by Bourgois,[*] alive at the time, so we called him and he gave us the name of a young man who gladly accepted and began translating the screenplay. A beautiful text and, hard to admit, very cheap. Publishers pay badly. He went on to work with us on two films and the texts were translated perfectly. However, one day Marianne met this young

---

[*] Christian Bourgois (1933-2007) founder of the publishing house Christian Bourgois Editeur

translator working in the street markets to make ends meet. It's a strange profession where different talents are not always given equal treatment. For our Chilean, we tracked down Roberto Bolaño's translator. He lives in the south of France, accepted the job and set to work. Halfway through, overwhelmed, he suggested that we entrust the second part of the translation to his brother. The failure was obvious: his translation had turned it into another text, another film.

Then, at the end, there remains the great show-down of egos, the finalisation of the credits, which bears no relation to peoples' roles in the film, the contracts, the reality of people's investment. No, it's something else. Let's call it the climax of the story, as screenwriters would say.

Post-production ends, but not production, and the principal producer, the lead producer, the one answerable to everyone and for everything, has the interminable task of finishing the film, drawing up the accounts, and harmonizing them between all the co-producers. We are responsible to all the institutions and partners who have entrusted us with their money. The journey is endless because the co-producers have already moved on. The figures fluctuate, get lost, get forgotten. New rules appear which we have never heard of before. We discover that one of the co-producers has never registered the film with his institution, and so on, ad infinitum. It all takes between eighteen months and five years, but no-one who sees the film will ever know, and so much the better for them.

Dispossession

And then comes the time of dispossession. A normal part of the process. A film does not tell, never tells, the story of its making. It lasts ninety minutes, perhaps a hundred, and it regains its complete freedom. It exists in its own right, and all the work put in, the risk taken to make it exist, disappears. Of course, we keep a few trivial rights and often, by the end of it, some debts. It is all very minimal and very little compared to what we had to do and live through for the film to exist.

And then this object, which has occupied us for so many months, must be entrusted to others, to others with the skills necessary for its future life—largely distributors and sellers. The good ones (we have the privilege of working with good people most of the time) take our little, unique treasure and welcome it into a large family. One film will swell a cohort of ten to twenty films per year and will be treated accordingly. And we will be put in our place. It becomes just one more film seeking exhibition. What it cost us in flesh and blood is irrelevant.

It takes its toll to watch the film go into distribution, to international sales, travelling from market to market, from festival to festival, but it is inevitable: other skills come into play. It's a difficult time, even more so when the film ends up in the wrong hands. Apart from some who defend the films to the bitter end, who have chosen them, how many just move on to the next one at the first sign of a mixed reception whilst freezing the rights they have. We have systematically fought to recover the rights to our films when they have been abandoned. It is impossible for a film-maker to simply accept that a film should be left to rot or die. We recover these rights, reissue the DVD and organise the film's circulation from within the means of our small organisation, small office—there are only two of us. Not to mention the sales agents who keep asking us for rights for twenty years, a way for them to build up a catalogue which they can monetise and which forces us to draw a definitive line under this creative work, a work which we have lived with so intimately.

But the most direct, brutal and very normal dispossession consists in giving back the film to its director. Once the film is finished, it is known only as the film "by": the author must reclaim everything. It is he/she who will live and travel with the film, it is he/she who goes on stage, it is his/her film. And we must, absolutely, give it back to them and grieve one more time. What is fascinating is that this reappropriation happens with each film and can be cruel, even humiliating, depending on the place and the role we have played for the film to exist. The more we have given, the more the troublesome witness must be buried, especially when the director has observed the scale of problems that we have had to sort out.

The way it happens is always the same, but it doesn't always happen in the same time frame. It almost always starts with minor, peripheral conflicts, conflicts that indicate the deep breath of recovery. With Marianne and I our eyes often meet, as if to say, "here we go." Ultimately, we will disappear, return the film to its owner and again, this is inevitable, perfectly normal: the author must reclaim his/her work. At this stage, the real question is the full appreciation of the significance of our intervention in giving birth to the work. The long immersion in creative collaboration often leads us to underestimate the role and nature of our contribution. In any case, this is what emerges at the end of each experience in the eyes of the filmmaker. There seems to be a profound osmosis which amounts to nothing more or less than the necessary journey between a filmmaker and his/her roots and history, and our own, which are quite different. We dream of fusion, but as Bataille* would say, there is only the question of discontinuity. Every film has a different story to tell, but these experiences are too painful to bring back to the surface.

We have taken twenty-one films to Cannes, eight to Venice, four to San Sebastian, two to Berlin, two to Locarno and one to Sundance. Thirty-eight high-level selections out of the forty-two feature films we have produced, thirty-two as principal producer and ten in co-production. Seventeen first works produced in twenty different countries. We have also produced seventy-five documentaries—but that's another huge story.

One in two films selected for Cannes. It's a great achievement, not often seen, and it's not always easy to understand and analyse the success which in each case is rooted in the selection of both a film and a filmmaker. To cut a long story short, first and foremost are the initial, meticulous choices, principle of which will always be the choice of the person who will carry the film, the director. However, beyond that, and this is where our role comes in, the determination to push the films to the very end: to carry them as high as they will go, to their greatest potential at all levels, without compromise, from the writing to the last stage of post-production. We never give up on anything. Above all we never reduce the film to its budget and we never act against the filmmaker. We do not believe that a film can be made against its director.

---

* Georges Bataille (1897-1962). French writer, philosopher and intellectual.

At the end of the journey, it also involves the tortuous, diabolical and cruel battle for selection by a major festival. You should definitely never produce "for Cannes," never fall into the trap of a risky and unsuitable schedule to be ready "for Cannes." Yet all these young filmmakers need "Cannes." It's a necessity to get out from the shadows, to have a chance to be seen (never guaranteed) and above all a chance to make a second film, and then others. We have a great responsibility—not to use a thousand and one false production pretexts just to push films through, to get them to the end. This is to condemn a filmmaker, a filmmaker's life, especially for a first film.

This lottery has its rules, being ready for Berlin in order to get a decision from Cannes. It works. We did it for Annemarie Jacir, for Patricio Guzman, and others, playing the festival sections against each other at the risk of getting our wings burnt.

With *Yalda*, this was a horror story. We love this film. We consider it strong and well achieved. Over time, with our experience, curiosity and presence on the festival circuit, we are usually able to judge and situate a film in the landscape. Of course we are probably a little too close, but *Yalda* is an exceptional film. It does take on a major challenge for cinema, that of being set in the framework of a television programme, which is a disadvantage. But Massoud pulls it off masterfully and the film is carried by two incredible, amazing actresses. We are almost ready for Berlin 2019, almost, because the film is still in post-production. It contains mock-ups for special effects, it is neither mixed nor graded. But it's a measure of how sure we are of our film that we are taking the risk of showing it at this stage. The film is on the "short list." We will never know who has viewed it and finally it is not selected, not even for a section parallel to the main competition. A strange feeling then sets in both for Massoud and for us. We begin to have doubts. How could we get it so wrong? We watch the films from Berlin, the ones from this year. We feel hurt, a little lost. We were not ready, so the film is more vulnerable than we thought. We will complete it for Cannes.

The first second film...

At the end of January, we come up against another challenge, probably the most painful in the history of this film. *A Respectable Family*, Massoud's first film, was banned in Iran. Unsurprisingly. It denounced the corruption of Ahmadinejad's regime with force and skill, and especially the extravagant business affairs of the guardians of the revolution, carried out behind the practical and modest mask of religion. When you walk around Tehran the contrast between the insolent luxury of the northern districts and the precariousness of the southern districts is astonishing. Even more surprising is the fact that there are more banks than all other businesses combined. So the film gets turned down. The list of pretexts is endless, starting with its insults to the Supreme Leader, and Massoud's journey into the wilderness will last for four years.

With *Yalda*, his legitimate obsession is to be able to show his film in his own country. In the past, the censors in Iran applied pressure by either giving or withholding permission to film. For *Yalda*, the script is scrutinised and finally accepted. The second level of censorship reveals itself in whether the film is, or is not, selected for the yearly national festival of Fajr. The festival has no real significance except that a film must participate in order to get the green light for exploitation in Iran. So, for Massoud, this is essential. We understand his passion and naturally share this dream of experiencing the film at its first screening with the Iranian audience. The film is selected. We prepare our suitcases once again. Being there, to return the film to its protagonists—in the country, the village, with the family where the film has been made—remains a fundamental experience in this profession.

I will never forget the screening of the film *Rice People* in Phnom Penh, in a large and beautiful hall overrun by vegetation and bats, with the whole village travelling in by bus to see themselves. The children ran up and down the aisles. The chaos was festive. The farmers laughed whenever they caught themselves on screen during a projection that lasted twice as long given the number of power cuts we suffered. We were the only ones to worry about this since, for the villagers, it was not only inevitable but it delightfully doubled the chance of catching themselves on screen.

In Tehran, it was just a nightmare. The film was placed in the category of first films: the previous one was simply erased. The press machine, ruthlessly controlled by the regime apart from a few independent cinephiles and marginals, had decided to destroy this "first" second film - to allow it but to destroy it. To cut a long story short, the press conference, where we were naively confident that we could defend the film, turned exclusively around the foreign money which we represented. It was a long nightmare exacerbated by the disassociation of the Iranian production team and some of the actresses under pressure from this campaign. But there was a striking perversity because at no time was the destruction of the film conducted on the political terrain. It was exclusively about the subject: only a bad film would make its audience sit through a television show when they would far prefer to watch it for real on television. Another hard, unfair, hurtful, humiliating journey.

Returning to earth, all we can do is dream about Cannes. And there, the same music as in Berlin, with just a little more discussion, and once again we are 'short listed' for the Official competition and the Directors Fortnight. They know us well and have done for years. Massoud's first film was in the Directors Fortnight and this one is much more accomplished. We are clear about this and can easily recognise when a film is not up to scratch, especially for this major festival. And it doesn't get through. We can't understand it. It's hard for us, but above all it is cruel and incomprehensible for its director. To leave nothing to chance, we submit it to be screened in parallel screenings at Cannes, and for the Locarno and Venice festivals, if only to increase the pressure on Cannes should one of these festivals decide, who knows, to accept if for their competition. And here the let-down is terrible. The film does not get through anywhere, incomprehensible. The exception, miraculously, comes with an enthusiastic email from the Americans, from Sundance. They are overwhelmed by the film and beg us to say no to everyone and hold back the film for January 2020. How to make sense of this? One can speculate about geopolitical interest but their enthusiasm is primarily about the cinematography. We have no difficulty in saying no to everyone. Contentment returns with the determination to keep going. Finally, Berlin 2020 likes the film and places it in a section compatible with the competition at Sundance. Happy ending?

Now begins the visa battle to enter the New World. We have been to Iran a few too many times for the Americans, a mere eight times, and for Massoud it is clearly much more complicated. Not impossible, except that Trump orders the assassination of General Soleimani,* straining relations between the two countries. At this point, if he wants to continue to live and work in his own country, it becomes impossible for Massoud to leave for the US. So, at the end of this long ordeal, Massoud will not be able to go to Sundance.

Each selection in these major festivals remains a challenge. There was a time when Gilles Jacob† could make a firm commitment to a film in July in the edit room. This was the case for the first film by Rithy Panh. Times have changed. The power of the selection panels over a film's life is immense and leads to cruel games right to the end, without mercy, even after the press conferences. With our most recent films the most painful experience involved our friend, the talented Chilean. For both his first and second film, the same disaster. The selection panel for Cannes' Sidebar, having shown a keen interest in the first ("It's one of our favourites," reads the text message) as well as in the second, drops the films at the very last stage. The second time this happens, they do it to make way for a Chilean director of greater notoriety, rejected for the Cannes' Official Competition. This director then slams the door in their face and opts for the Directors Fortnight. The devastation for a young filmmaker. Eventually, with no discredit, both films do get selected for the Competition in San Sebastian.

It's a Thursday. Massoud calls us. It's still confidential but we have won the Grand Prix at Sundance.

---

* Qasem Soleimani, Iranian Major General assassinated by American drone strike, January 3rd 2020
† Critic, essayist, since 1978 magnificent general delegate of Cannes Festival, then President 2001 – 2014

This is an immense joy. Yes, it's only a small film and a small festival in the depths of Utah, but at one stroke it's an act of faith: a scathing response to all those who don't believe in this film, an infinite joy for the actresses who gave their all, and the impressive discovery of the young Sadaf. It's also the revelation of a great filmmaker and, for us, the end of this story and the beginning of another one, one without precedent.

January 2020. A virus assails China. In Berlin, there are thousands of us mingling, rubbing shoulders—we kiss a lot in this business. The market is buzzing. Covid has evidently not arrived. Even so, we still have the greatest difficulty getting our Iranian actresses and our actor to travel. Incredibly, and at vast cost, we make it. The leading actress only gets a visa for the 25th. The official date for the screening is the 23rd. We keep trying and decide to bring her over for the final screenings and then, day by day, the travel companies close all flights from Teheran. Iran is a country particularly badly affected. In the end Sadaf doesn't make it. Even worse, she gives up on attending the first three major festivals. Eventually they also get cancelled. Everything else follows in the same direction. The film's release is postponed to the autumn, a hypothetical date. The epic adventure of this film has reached its climax. Another era blows in.

Sant Climent Sescebes, June 2021

Alan Fountain (Channel 4), Thierry Garrel (Arte),
Eckart Stein (ZDF)

The brigade of militant cinema, early years

Mohamed Afarideh, Producer of *A Respectable Family*, his son, Kazem, and Massoud on the immortal CROISETTE, Cannes 2010.

With the hypothetical producer of dreams, Tehran 2019

Tehran Hotel Room – 'indescribable kitsch, sticky carpets, above the noisiest crossroad of an urban motorway.'

Sadaf Asgari, wonderful actress of *Yalda*, out on the town with
Marianne whilst Jacques Bidou and Jacques Comets,
the film's editor, reinvent the world.

With Fernando de Santiago, in Chile.

Marianne and Pablo, in Patagonia.

Plotting with Pascal Bonitzer and Raoul Peck, two masters of
cinema, for a film which never finally gets made.

Marianne and I with Danilo Caputo, San Sebastian & Venice.
At film festivals it usually rains.

.....and forty films later.

BIOGRAPHY – JACQUES BIDOU

Chaotic period of studies, inclined to show more interest in horses and music than in school. Philosophy Baccalaureate. He heads for l'IDHEC, Institut Des Hautes Etudes Cinématographique, which later becomes La Fémis after l'IDHEC goes through years of crisis in the run up to 1968. The history teachers are drawn to a new school in Brussels, INSAS, The Belgian National Institute for Visual Arts, Communication and Technology. Suzanne Baron, Ghislain Cloquet, Pierre Lhomme, Michel Fano join Delvaux, Ravar, in Belgium. Two years of studies in exceptional conditions.

Called upon to take over the editing of François Reichenbach's Soy Mexico, he dives in and drowns: too immature to succeed despite the benevolent help of Chris Marker and Carlos Fuentes. He befriends Ruy Guerra and proposes to Marker that he join the project Loin du Vietnam, (Far from Vietnam) 1968, illumination, the revolution in progress. One of a group of five, he starts showing films in occupied factories. This experience gives rise to the desire to produce films that can make a political intervention.

Marginalised by the still nascent broadcast television, they are lulled by the great dream of alternative power. With the group that came out of 1968, he creates Dynadia, which quickly attracts a good number of technicians and directors, then Unicite, which he directs for 10 years.

1982 Development Director of Communications for Mutuelles de France. 1984 creation of JBA (with Jean Bayle, same initials), a design company for press relations, and from 1987 to 2021 JBA Production, which gives birth to 114 films (documentary and fiction).
cf filmography www.jbaproduction.com

Instructor
From 1988 to 1996 President of Ateliers Varan. From 1998 to 2011 on the Executive Board of La Femis and Vice-President (France) from 95 to 98. From 1990 to 1999 tutor and consultant, EAVE (European Audiovisual Entrepreneurs).

1995 to 2000 Director of Studies for programme "Produire en Region, France." 1999 - 2017 Creator and Director of Studies for Eurodoc (European Media Programme). 2011 & 2012 Director of Studies of Docmed (Euromed Audiovisual Programme). 2017 to 2021 Pedagogics team and tutor, Eurodoc.

Actor
Lead role in Monday Morning by Otar Iosseliani, Silver Bear, Best Direction, Berlin 2002
JBA PRODUCTION • 1987/2024
www.jbaproduction.com

FILMOGRAPHY – JBA PRODUCTION
FEATURE FILMS

1989
NEITHER WITH GOD OR THE DEVIL by Nilo Peirera del Mar • First feature
Co-production JBA / Channel 4
Awards: Special Price of Jury, Cartagena Festival, Colombia 1990

1990
TINPIS RUN by Pengau Nengo • First feature
First feature from Papua New Guinea
Co-production JBA / La Sept Arte / Channel 4 / TV Drama
Special mention by Fipresci, Rotterdam Film Festival, 1991/ Best Actor, Balafon Film Festival

1992
THE DEVIL'S CHILDREN by Claude Timon Gaignaire
Co-production JBA / France 3 / TV3 Catalunya / ZDF

1993
RICE PEOPLE by Rithy Panh • First feature
Budget 1 601 083 Euros/ Co-production JBA / France / La Sept Cinéma / Thelma Film / Switzerland
Awards: Official Selection in competition, Festival de Cannes 1994 / Prize of Ecumenical Jury, Singapore, 1995/ Prize for Best Actress (Peng Phanin the role of the mother) & Special Mention by Jury/ Special Jury Prize, Prize, Hawaii 1995

1993

BAB EL OUED CITY by Merzak Allouache

Budget 1 117 886 Euros / Co-production JBA / Les Matins Films / La Sept Cinéma / Flash Back (Algeria) France 52% / Algeria 48% / Awards: Selection for Cannes Festival, 1994 Un Certain Regard/ International Critics Prize and Glaces Gervais Festival Award, Cannes/ Grand Prize IMA 2e Biennale of Arab Cinema/ Silver « R » Riminicinema / Tanit d'Argent & Utica Prize, Carthage/ Olivier d'Argent & Prize for Best Music, Bastia Festival, Corsica.

1993

XIME by Sana Na N'hada • First feature

Co-production JBA France / Molenwiek Nederland

Awards: Official selection Un Certain regard Cannes 1994

1995

HEY COUSIN ! by Merzak Allouache

Budget 2 568 960 Euros

Co-production JBA / La Sept Cinéma / Artémis / RTBF / France 80% / Benelux 20% /

Awards: Selection by Festival de Cannes for Directors' Fortnight 1996 / Arab Critics Prize / Vevey Youth Jury Award, Beilinzone, Switzerland 1996/ Golden Anchor Award, Haifa / Golden Tanit Award, OUA Prize & special mention at FIPRESCI Festival de Carthage / Golden Bayard Award, Festival de Namur/ M'NET Film Awards South Africa / Prize for Best Screenplay and Best Director, Cairo Film Festival / Silver Pyramid, Béziers Film Festival, special Mention of the Prize for Interpretation for Gad Elmaleh and Mess Hattou / Interpretation Prize (Mess Hattou) & Best Film Montereau 1997.

1995

ARISTOTLE'S PLOT by Jean-Pierre Bekolo

Budget 309 944 € / Television Drama

Co-production JBA / British Film Institute / Framework International / France / UK /

Prize for Best Sound, Fespaco 1997

1995

FOOLS by Ramadan Suleman • First feature

Budget 954 725 Euros / Co-production JBA / Natives at Large / Framework Int / Ebano / MNET / France / South Africa / Mozambique / Zimbabwe

Awards : Silver Lion Locarno Film Festival 1997 / Prize for interpretation (Male) , Balafon

1995
FLAME de Ingrid Sinclair • First feature
Co-production JBA / Black and White, Simon Bright (Zimbabwe)
Awards : Directors' Fortnight, Cannes Film Festival, 1996

1995
DANCE OF THE WIND by Rajan Khosa • First feature
Co-production JBA / Pandora Films, Karl Baumgartner (Germany)
Awards: Official selection Venice Film Festival 1997

1996
CORPS PLONGES by Raoul Peck
Budget 1 139 857 € / Television Drama / Co-production : JBA / La
Sept Arte / Velvet Film /
Awards : Selection for Festival Racines Noires, Montréal, Toronto /
Cinéma Tous Ecrans, Geneva / Haïfa Film Festival / London Film
Festival / Margaret Mead Film Festival / Namur Film Festival /
Cairo Film Festival / Balafon Film Festival

1996
ONE EVENING AFTER THE WAR by Rithy Panh
Budget 2 415 153 Euros / Co-production JBA / Thelma Film AG
(Swiss) / La Sept Cinéma / Cambodian Center of Cinema / CMC
(Belgium) / DRS (Swiss) France 80% / Swiiss & Germany 20%
Awards : Official Selection, Un Certain Regard, Cannes Festival,
1998

1997
THE MUTANTS by Teresa Villaverde
Budget 1 770 328 Euros / Co-production: JBA / Mutante Filmes
(Portugal) / La Sept Cinéma / Pandora Film / Arte ZDF / RTP
(Portugal) / France & Germany 49% / Portugal 51%
Awards: Official Selection Un Certain Regard, Cannes 1998 / Prize
for Support for Cinema Distribution of Quality Films, Belgium,
Cine Decouverte, 1998 / Prize for Best Actress (Female), Ana
Moreira Festival of Taormina / United Nations Prize for 50th
Anniversary of Human Rights, Med Film Festival; Bastia Festival
/ Grand Prize of Jury OCIC / Special Mention, Ana Moreira Inde-
pendent Film Festival, Buenos Aires 1999 / Official selection for
Portugal at OSCARS, 2000

1997
SHADOWS IN THE NIGHT by Pankaj Butalia • First feature
Co-production: JBA / Vital Films /Pankaj Butalia (Inde) /
Official selection at Venice Film Festival 1999

1999
THOMAS IN LOVE by Pierre Paul Renders • First feature
Co-production : JBA / Entre Chien et Loup, Diana Elbaum
(Belgium)
Awards : Venice Film Festival, 2000

1999
LUMUMBA by Raoul Peck
Budget 4 262 102 Euros / Co-production JBA / Arte France
Cinéma / Entre Chien et Loup / Essential Film Production / RTBF
/ Libérator productions / France 70% / Belgium 20% / Allemagne
10% Awards : Directors' Fortnight Cannes 2000 / Prize at Festival
de Saint-Domingue 2001 / Best Film, Pan African Film, Beverley
Hills / Best Feature, Fespaco 2001 / Prize for the Diaspora, 11th
African Film Festival, Milan & Audience Prize of City of Milan /
Best Actor, Eriq Ebouaney & Grand Prize OCIC Human Rights
Watch International Film Festival, USA / Irène Diamond Lifetime
Achievement Award for Raoul Peck, Acapulco Black Film Festival
/ Filmmaker Trophy, 5th Encounter of Latin American Cinema,
Lima and Fellini Prize awarded by UNESCO, Prize from the Epis-
copal Conference, Peru

1999
BACK DOOR by Yorgos Tsemberopoulos
Co-production: JBA / Ideefixe Productions / Fenia Cossovitsa
(Grèece)

2000
APRIL CAPTAINS by Maria de Medeiros • First feature
Budget 5 135 148 € / Co-production JBA / Mutante Filmes /
Filmart / Alia Film / Arte France Cinéma / France 2 Cinéma / RTP
(Portugal) / France 50% / Portugal 20% / Espagne 20% / Italie
10%
Awards : Official Selection, Un Certain Regard, Cannes 2000 /
Audience Prize, Arcachon Festival / Audience Prize, Cinessone
France 2001 / Best Film, 24th International Festival of São Paulo

2001
PAU AND HIS BROTHER by Marc Recha
co-production JBA / Oberon Cinematografica, Antonio Chavarrias (Spain)/ Spain 70% / France 30% Awards : Official Selection, Cannes Festival in Competition, 2001

2002
A PIECE OF SKY by Bénédicte Liénard • First feature
Budget 2 066 480 Euros/ Co-production; JBA / Tarantula Belgium / Tarantula Luxembourg / ARTE France / France 2 Cinéma / RTBF / France 50% / Bénélux 50%
Awards: Official Selection, Un Certain Regard Cannes 2002 / Best Actor (Female) for Séverine Caneele Bafici , Argentina 2003

2003
FEATHERS IN MY HEAD by Thomas de Thier • First feature
Budget 2 053 347 Euros / Co-production JBA / Magellan Production & Consulting / ARTE France / RTBF / 47th Parallel / France 74% / Belgique 26%
Awards : Directors Fortnight, Cannes 2003

2003
WHERE IS MADAME CATHERINE ? by Marc Recha
Budget 2.681.067 Euros / Co-production : JBA / Eddie Saeta / France 52% / Spain 48%
Awards : Official Selection, Un Certain Regard, Cannes 2003 / Special Jury Prize & Grand Prize for Best Screenplay 2002, with support from Fujifilm

2004
SALVADOR ALLENDE by Patricio Guzman
Budget 854.783 Euros/ Feature Documentary / Co-production: JBA / Les Films de la Passerelle / Mediapro / CV Films / University of Gadalajara / Patricio Guzman Productions/ France 58% / Belgique 20% / Espagne 12% / Allemagne 10%
Awards : Official Selection, Out of Competition, Cannes Festival, 2004 / Best Documentary Prize, Lima; Salvador Allende Prize at Trieste Festival; First Prize Alsace, for European Documentary, Strasbourg

2005
ZULU LOVE LETTER by Ramadan Suleman
Budget 1.985.321 Euros / Co-production: JBA / Hollybell / Natives
at large / ZDF Arte / France 55% / South Africa 45%
Awards: Official Selection Venice Film Festival 2004 / Silver Tanit,
Carthage Film Festival 2004 / Grand Prize, Mons Festival 2005 /
Special Prize, European Union, Best Actress (female) for Pamela
Nomvete Marimbe, UNICEF Prize for the Promotion of Women's
Rights, 9th Prize of L'Inalco at the Fespaco Festival (Burkina Faso)
/ Best Feature Prize, Festival for African Cinema, Angers, 2005 /
Best Actor for Mpumi Malatsi, Capetown World Cinema Festival

2007
SALT OF THIS SEA by Annemarie Jacir • First feature
Budget 1.279.770 € / Co-production: JBA / Philistine Films /
Thelma Film AG / Tarantula / Louverture Films / Clarity World
Film / Augustus Film / TSR / Mediapro / France 34% / Suisse 24%
/ Espagne 20% / Belgique 12% / Holland 10%
Awards: Official Selection, Un Certain Regard Cannes 2008 /
Special Jury and International Critics Award, International Festival
of Asiatic and Arab Cinema, India, 2008 / Best Screenplay, Inter-
national Film Festival, Dubai / Randa Chahal Prize, Journées
Cinématographiques de Carthage / Best Film, Sguardi Altrove Film
Festival / Audience Prize for Best Film, Chicago Palestine Film
Festival 2009 / Best Actress (Female), Euro-Arab Film Festival,
Amal / The Audience Choice Award, International Festival of
Human Rights, New Orleans, 2010

2007
SALAMANDRA by Pablo Agüero • First feature
Budget 1.084.521 Euros/ Television Drama / Co-production JBA /
Rohfilm / Rizoma / France 78% / Germany 12% / Argentina 10%
Awards : Directors Fortnight, Cannes 2008

2009
FACE by Tsai Ming-Liang
Budget 3.825.411 Euros / Co-production: JBA / Homegreen Films
/ Louvre Museum / Arte France Cinéma / Tarantula / Circe Films /
RTBF / France 67% / Taiwan 12% / Belgium 10%/ Holland 10%
Awards: Official Selection, in Competition Cannes, 2009 / Best
Costume & Design, Golden Horse Festival, Taiwan, 2009 / Best
Costume & Design 4th Asian Film Awards AFA, Hong-Kong,
2010

2010
CORPO CELESTE by Alice Rohrwacher • First feature
Co-production: JBA / Tempesta / Italie 70% / France 20% / Switzerland 10%
Awards: Selection Directors Fortnight, Cannes 2011/ Silver Ribbon Award, Rome City /Best First Feature, Taormina Film Festival 2011

2012
A RESPECTABLE FAMILY by Massoud Bakhshi • First feature
Budget 786.171 Euros/ Co-production : JBA / Firoozei Films / France 62% / Iran 38%
Awards : Selection Directors Fortnight, Cannes 2012 / Black Pearl Award New Horizons, Abu Dhabi

DOG FLESH by Fernando Guzzoni • First feature
Budget 417.235 Euros / Co-production: JBA / Ceneca producciones / Chile 50%/ France 40% / Germany 10%
Awards: Selection, New Directors, Festival de San Sebastian, Best Film, San Sebastian 2012 / The Ingmar Bergman Award, Goteborg Festival / Best Film, Festival de Valdivia / Best First Feature, Havana Festival / Best Actor Punta del Este / Rail D'Oc Festival de Toulouse

2012
THE REPENTANT by Merzak Allouache
Co-production: JBA / Baya Films / Algeria 80% / France 20%
Awards: Directors Fortnight, Cannes 2012 / Label Europa Cinéma / Best Actress for Adila Bendimerad & Best Actor for Khaled Benaissa, Festival d'Angoulême / Special Mention, Silver Hugo Award, International Film Festival Festival Chicago / Asfaan award for works of Merzak Allouache, Festival of African Cinema, Cordoba / Golden Goddess for Best Actor to Nabil Asli, Festival of Prishtina / Best Screenplay, International Film Festival of Addis Abeba / Award for Artistic Expression to Adila Bendimerad, Roma Film Festival / Best Narrative Feature Film Award, Doha Tribeca Film Festival / Best Actress for Adila Bendimerad at 35th International Festival of Cairo / Fipresci Prize for BestFilm, International Festival Kerala / Award for outstanding achievement in cinematography for Mohamed Tayeb El Aggoun, Scarborough Film Festival, Toronto.

2012

VIRGIN MARGARIDA by Licinio Azevedo • First feature
Co-production: JBA / Ebano Multimedia Ltd / Mozambique /
Portugal/ France
Awards : Selection Toronto Festival / Best Supporting Actor for
Iva Mugalela, Carthage JCC 2012 / Audience Award and Special
Mention of the "Signis" Jury for humanitarian values, Festival
d'Amiens / Audence Prize, Festival of African Cinema, Angers 2013
/ Best Supporting Actress for Hermelinda Simela, Movie Academy
Awards / Prize for Intercultural Communication,and Best Actress
for Iva Mugalela, International Festival Vues d'Afrique, Canada
2013 / Audience Award, Angers Festival 2014

2013

THE ROOFTOPS by Merzak Allouache
Budget 382.528 Euros / Co-production : JBA / Baya Films / France
66% / Algeria 34%
Awards : Selection for Competition, Venice 2013 / Best Director for
Arab World and Fipresci Award, Abu Dhabi Festival / Filmaker of
the Year, Variety Magazine / Golden Amayas, Alger Film Festival
of Maghrebian Cinema

2013

STRAY DOGS by Tsaï Ming-Liang
Co-production : JBA / Homegreen Films / Taïwan / France
Awards : Selection in Competition, Jury Prize Venice 2013

2014

CAIN'S BROTHER by Marcell Gerö • First feature documentary
Budget 479.540 Euros/ Co-production: JBA / Campfilm / Arte
France / France 70% / Hungary 30%
Awards: Selection for New Directors Competition, San Sebastian
Spain / Prize, 11th Verzio International Human Rights Documen-
tary Film Festival, Budapest 2014 / Best Human Rights Documen-
tary Special Award awarded by the Student Jury 11th Golden Eye
Festival Budapest / Best Documentary in 2014 awarded by the
Hungarian Film Critics' Association 2015 / 11th Zagreb Dox Inter-
national Documentary Film Festival, Zagreb, Croatia, 2015 / "Big
Stamp" Award for Best Film in Regional Competition 25th Medi-
awave International Film Festival, Komárom / Best feature length
documentary, 14th Doxa Documentary Film Festival, Vancouver /
Honorable mention of the jury & Golden Eye Prize for best cinematography, Georgia 2015 / Prix Docuthriller DoxDF (Mexico)

2016
EVA DOESN'T SLEEP de Pablo Agüero
Budget: 1.039.730 Euros / Co-production JBA / Haddock Films / Tornasol / France 60% / Argentina 30% / Espagne 10%
Awards: Selection for Competition at San Sebastian Film Festival 2015 (Spain) / Best Cinematography, Festival de Mar del Plata 2015 / Best Film, Festival d'Amiens / Best Film Pinamar Film Festival / Prix Ciné+ and Prix Cinema in Construction, Toulouse Festival / 5 Silver Condors Argentina 2016, Best Direction, Best Photography, Best Artistic Direction, Best Costume, Best Sound

2016
JESUS by Fernando Guzzoni
Budget 630.624 Euros / Co-production: JBA / Rampante Films / Una Film / Graal Films / Burning Blue / France 36,68% / Chile including Colombia 34,51% / Germany 17,62% / Greece 11,19%
Awards: Selection for Competition, San Sebastian Festival 2016 / Best Actor, Torino Film Festival / Best Actor and Best Editing, Ficsur, Argentina

2017
WAJIB by Annemarie Jacir
Co-production : JBA / Philistine Films / Palestine/ France
Awards: Selection Competition Locarno 2017 / Don Quijote Prize from International Federation of Film Clubs / Premio Prize for Environment & Quality of Life, Jury of Giovani / ISPEC Cinema Prize, Institute for Contemporary History & Philosophy, Locarno / Best Film & Best Actors, Dubai International Film Festival / Best Film et Best Actor, Argentine Critics award & SiGNIS Award, Mar del Plata / Special Mention of Jury, London BFI Film Festival / Best Film, International Film Festival of Kerala / Best Film - Golden Unicorn & Audience Award, Amiens International Film Festival / Jury Prize, MedFilm / Youth Jury Award, Cinemed / Coup de Cœur Award, Festival of Cinema, Pays de Fayenc / Best Actor, Fest of International Mediterranean Cinema, Tétouan / Audience Award for Middle east, Florence / Circle Award, Washington DC International Film Festival / Best Film, Best Screnplay & Best actor, Arab Critics 2018 / Best Film, Film Festival of Ibea / Best European Film, Prishtina International Film Festival / Best Film, Casablanca Film Festival / Jury Prize & Best Actor, Oran Film Festival / Best Film, Cinetopia Film Festival / Best Film, Kraniska Gora International / Best Narrative Feature, Mizna Arab Film Fest Minneapoli / Best Film & Critics Award, Malmo Arab Film Festival / Best Perfor-

mance for Mohammed Bakri, Jerusalem Int Film Festival of Gaza /
Audience Award, International Film Festival of Algeria

2018
DONBASS by Sergei Loznitsa
Co-production: Majade, Arthouse Traffic, JBA Production,
Digital Cube, Graniet Film, Wild at Art / Allemagne 46,94% /
Ukraine 22,31% / France 10,53% / Rumania 10,20% / Holland
10,02% Awards : Selection for Opening, Un Certain Regard,
Cannes 2018 and Prize for Art Direction/ Giraldillo d'Or, Euro-
pean Film Festival, Seville / Alexandre-Dovjenko Prize, Best Film,
Best Director, Best Screenplay : 3 Golden Dziga Awards by the
Ukrainian Film Academy 2019

2020
YALDA, A NIGHT FOR FORGIVENESS by Massoud Bakhshi
Budget: 1.311.450 Euros / Co-production: JBA / Close Up Film /
Niko Film / Amour Fou / Ali Mossafa / France 45,61% / Germany
32,25% / Switzerland 11,61% / Luxembourg 10,53%
Awards: Grand Prize Jury Sundance 2020 / Berlinale Genera-
tion14+ / Best Screenplay, Sofia Film Festival / Best Director,
Antalya / Circle Award, Washington / ELLE magazine readers'
Prize / Screenplay Prize, Barcelona Film Festival 2021

2021
SOW THE WIND by Danilo Caputo
Budget 1.135.140 Euros / Co-production: JBA / Okta Film / Graal
Films / Italy 69,99%/ France 17,61% / Greece 12,40%
Awards: Selection for Berlinale Panorama, 2020

DOCUMENTARIES

1988
SOUTH AFRICAN CHRONICLES by Varan Workshop of
Johannesburg—90' / La Sept
Awards : Grand Prize Festival of Video Reality, Brussels / First
Prize, Cinéma du Réel

1988
OANA, AN ADOLESCENT by Nicole André - 40' / La Sept
Arte

1988
HERE AND THERE by Michael Hoare—60' / La Sept Arte
Award : International Prize for Television, Geneva Rencontres
Medias Nord

1988
BUENOS AIRES CRONICAS VILLERAS by Cespedes and
Carmen Guarini—75'
Awards : Selection at Cine Ojo & Cinéma du Réel

1989
LA CARRESE de Giorgio di Nella—60' / La Sept Arte
Awards : Enrico Fulchignoni Prize, 8th Bilan of Ethnographic Film
/ Golden Blaise, Festival de Valbonne

1989
THE HINTERLAND by Guy Olivier—60' / La Sept Arte /
France 3 / Cinéma du Réel

1989
MEXICO, THE THREE EARTHQUAKES by Ernesto Rimoch
and Eva Saraga—51' / Channel 4

1989
CHERRY ; PHYSIOLOGY OF A DISTILLATION by Miroslav
Sebestik—45' / La Sept Arte / Mikros

1989
SITE 2 by Rithy Panh—90 & 60' / ZDF / La Sept Arte / INA
Awards : Grand Prize for Documentary by la Scam 1989 / Grand
Prize for Documentary, Festival of Amiens, 1989

1989
YOUR EYES BIGGER THAN YOUR EARS by Jean Arlaud—
45' / La Sept Arte

1990
CHAPARE by Daniele Incalcaterra—90' / Channel 4 / La Sept
Arte
Awards : Jury Prize, Latin American Festival, Biarritz / Cinéma du
Réel

1990
FROM THE TREE TO THE VIOLIN by Vincent Blanchet—60'
/ La Sept Arte

1990
YASSER ARAFAT, ITINERARY by Yves Loiseau—60' / TF1 /
La Sept Arte / Ina

1991
REMEMBERING ROMERO by Peter ChappelL - 45' / Channel
4 / La Sept Arte / Television Espanola / Radio Telefis Eireann

1991
LANDSCAPES : BIERRE LES SEMUR by Jean-Loïc Portron—
27' / La Sept Arte / Ina

1992
SALUDEMOS by Cécile Patingre—60' / Fémis / Eictv

1992
LISTEN by Miroslav Sebestik—140' / La Sept Arte / Sacem /
Mikros / Centre Pompidou

1992
LANDSCAPES: PORTE DE BAGNOLET by Pierre Zucca—27'
/ La Sept Arte / Ina

1992
LANDSCAPES : FOS SUR MER by Jean-Loïc Portron—26' / La
Sept Arte / Ina

1992
LANDSCAPES : TREIS KARDEN by Jean-Loïc Portron—26' /
La Sept Arte / Ina

1993
PERMANENT ADRESS by Cécile Patingre and Anne Peyregne—
50' / La Sept Arte / Fémis

1993
LANDSCAPES : CAMPELLO ALTO by Jean-Loïc Portron—26'
/ La Sept Arte / Ina

1994
LANDSCAPES : CARCHUNA by Jean-Loïc Portron—26' / La Sept Arte / Ina

1994
LANDSCAPES : SAINT GILLES DE LA RÉUNION by Radha Jaganathen—24' / La Sept Arte / Ina

1994
TALES FROM A HARD CITY by Kim Flitcroft—75' / La Sept Arte / Channel 4 / Picture Palace North
Awards : Grand Prix, International Festival, Marseille / Best Film, Indies Awards, London

1994
DANCE OF THE MONKEY AND THE FISH by Pierre-Alain Meier—41' / ZDF / Thelma Film

1994
WHAT IS TO BE DONE ? by André Van In—60' / France3 / Ina / Archipel33

1994
WHAT IS TO BE DONE, BIS ? by André Van In—60' / France3 / Ina / Archipel33

1994
ONE WAY, THREE STORIES FROM RIO DE LA PLATA by Nadine Fischer, Noël Burch and Nelson Scartaccini—83' / La Sept Arte / Ina

1995
LANDSCAPES : HEBDEN BRIDGE by Jean-Loïc Portron—26' / La Sept Arte / Ina

1995
GIPSY FAIR WITH THE PININI by carole Fierz—28'

1995
THE RESTITUTION by Catherine Zins—93' / La Sept Arte / Ceska Televise

1995
PEOPLE FROM THE SHANTYTOWNS by Robert Bozzi—88'
/ La Sept Arte
Prize of the best creative documentary Scam 96

1995
MY VOTE IS MY SECRET by July Henderson, Thulani Mokoena,
Donne Rundle—95' / La Sept Arte

1996
LANDSCAPES: BITCHE by Jean-Loïc Portron —25' / La Sept
Arte / Ina

1996
LANDSCAPES : LORIENT by Jean-Loïc Portron—26' / La Sept
Arte / Ina

1996
LANDSCAPES : PORTEL by Jean-Loïc Portron—27' / La Sept
Arte / Ina

1996
FAUSTO COPPI AN ITALIAN STORY by Jean-Christophe
Rosé—90 & 52'
La Sept Arte / TSI (Switzerland) / Istituto Luce (Italy)
Awards Silver Palm, International Festival of Sports Film, Palermo,
1996 / Best Sports Programme, 18th Festival of Television, BANFF
1997

1996
INÈS MY SISTER by Carole Fierz—50'

1996
ALURICAN / Périphérie / Segona Unitat / Festival Cinéma du
Réel 1996
Awards: Best Creative Documentary, 11th Festival of Gentilly

1997
LANDSCAPES : AUXEY-DURESSES by Jean-Loïc Portron—
26' / La Sept Arte / Ina

1997
LANDSCAPES : VAL D'HERENS by Jean-Loïc Portron—26' /
La Sept Arte / Ina

1997
LANDSCAPES : ISLAND OF SYMI by Jean-Loïc Portron—28'
/ La Sept Arte / Ina

1997
VOYAGES, VOYAGES : SCOTLAND by Jean-Loïc Portron—
43' / La Sept Arte

1997
DEAR CATHERINE by Raoul Peck—19' / Velvet Films

1997
OUR FRIENDS AT THE BANK by Peter Chappell—75'
La Sept Arte / Yle / Channel 4 / Danmark radio / Sbs / Ikon / Svt
Awards: Silver Fipa « Grands reportages» 1998 / Mention in «
Section Screens Nord/Sud Section, Festival Vues d'Afrique Festival,
Montréal 1998 / Libraries Jury Prize - Cinéma du Réel 1998 /
Okomedia Prize for Best Journalist Direction, Germany, 1998

1997
LANDSCAPES : ETRETAT by Jean-Loïc Portron—26' / La Sept
Arte / Ina

1997
VOYAGES, VOYAGES : LAC LÉMAN by Pierre-Yves Moulin
- 42' / La Sept Arte

1998 THE MEDELLIN NOTEBOOKS by Catalina Villar—75' /
La Sept Arte / Entre Chien et Loup
Awards : Feature Documentary and Audience Prize, Festival de
Nyon 1998 / Prize for Best Feature Documentary, Festival Amas-
cultura, Portugal / Documentary Prize from La Semaine Interna-
tionale, Santiago

1998
VOYAGES, VOYAGES : NAMIBIA by Rina Sherman—42' / La
Sept Arte

1998
LANDSCAPES : SISTERON by Jean-Loïc Portron—27' / La Sept
Arte / Ina

1998
VOYAGES, VOYAGES : ROBINSON CRUSOE ISLAND by
Patricio Guzmán—42' / La Sept Arte

1998
JUSTICE by Olivier Ballande—58' / Unité de programme RFO /
Entre Chien et Loup
Awards : Michel Mitrani Prize, FIPA 1999 / Special Mention,
French Cinema, Cinéma du Réel France1999 / Ebel Prize, Inter-
national Competition of Independants / Special Mention Prix de la
Jeunesse, Rencontres Médias Nord/Sud 99 / Bronze Prize, Media
Net Award, 1999

1999
LANDSCAPES : EISENHUTTENSTADT by Jean-Loïc
Portron—28' / La Sept Arte / Ina

1999
LANDSCAPES : TROMSØ by Jean-Loïc Portron—28' / La Sept
Arte / Ina

1999
VOYAGES, VOYAGES : NORWAY by Jean-Loïc Portron—42'
/ La Sept Arte

1999
VOYAGES, VOYAGES : NORTHERN TUNISIA by Pierre-
Yves Moulin—42' / La Sept Arte

2000
LANDSCAPES : ISTANBUL by Jean-Loïc Portron—28' / ARTE
France / Ina

2000
VOYAGES, VOYAGES : VIENTIANE by Didier Nion—42' /
ARTE France

2000
MY AMERICAN FAMILY by Robert Bozzi—France 3 / Rtbf

2000
RHYTHMS OF RAJASTHAN by Michel Marre—40' / ARTE
France

2000
THE PROFIT AND NOTHING BUT by Raoul Peck—57' /
ARTE France / RTBF (Belgium) / Entre Chien et Loup (Belgium)

2000
WOMEN OF HEZBOLLAH by Maher Abi Samra—52' / ARTE
France / RTBF (Belgium)

2001
PARIS TAXI by Robert Bozzi—51' / France 3, France 5, Forum
des Images

2001
VOYAGES, VOYAGES : MADRID by Patricio Guzmán—41' /
ARTE France

2004
GOD, DOLLAR, FLAG AND DOG by Robert Bozzi—52' /
France 5

2005
FUCKING SHEFFIELD by Kim Flitcroft—75' / Picture Palace
North, ARTE France

2005
NOTES FROM A KURDISH REBEL by Stefano Savona—78' /
ARTE France
Awards : Prize from la Scam / Special Mention, Youth Jury Festival
du Réel 2006

2009
HEUREUX QUI CONNUT NICE de Robert Bozzi—52' /
France 3 Marseille / France 3 National

2010
ENERGUMEN by Jean-Loïc Portron / Feature Documentary—77'
Production : JBA / ARTE GIE
Ouverture des Rendez-Vous de l'Histoire de Blois (14 Octobre 2010)

2010
FLOWERS IN THE MIRROR, MOON IN THE WATER by François Lunel—47' / Louvre Museum

2016
SOWETO, TIMES OF WRATH by Siphamandla Bongwana, Jerry Obakeng Gaegane, Standford Gipson, Nduduzo Shandu—60' / Arte France

www.ingramcontent.com/pod-product-compliance
Ingram Content Group UK Ltd.
Pitfield, Milton Keynes, MK11 3LW, UK
UKHW020309130525
5863UKWH00064B/529